P9-CIW-978

Knitting Motifs
for Babies and Kids

Lucinda Guy

Knitting Motifs for Babies and Kids

Lucinda Guy

Illustrations by François Hall

TRAFALGAR SQUARE
North Pomfret, Vermont

First published in the United States of America in 2010 by
Trafalgar Square Books
North Pomfret, Vermont 05053

Motif design and text copyright © Lucinda Guy 2010
Illustration, chart, diagram and photography
copyright © François Hall 2010

Copyright Berry & Bridges © 2010

All rights reserved.
No part of this book may be reproduced, stored in a
retrieval system, or transmitted in any form or by any
means electronic, electrostatic, magnetic tape,
mechanical, photocopying, recording or otherwise,
without prior permission in writing of the publisher.

Designer François Hall
Editor Katie Hardwicke

Library of Congress Control Number: 2009937624

ISBN 978-1-57076-459-2

Reproduced in the UK
Printed in Singapore

10 9 8 7 6 5 4 3 2 1

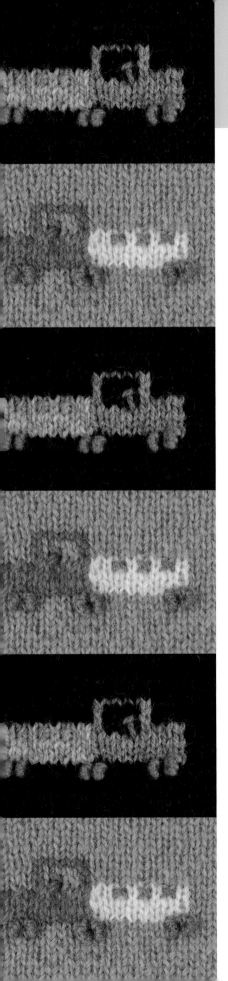

Contents

Introduction

A single knitted motif can make a plain and simple child's garment look instantly more charming and individual. A baby's jacket can be transformed if a sweet little mouse motif is repeated around the border or a small boy's sweater can be made more fun to wear if it has a big, colorful robot marching across it. Motifs can be placed wherever you want them and on all kinds of knitwear; they can appear as bands of pattern on a tank top, as individual squares of a patchwork blanket, as patterned patch pockets on dresses, in pride of place as a single motif on a favorite sweater or hat, or on knitted bags, purses, and even pencil cases.

Often only very small amounts of colored yarn are needed to knit the motif, so it is an ideal way to use up odds and ends of your favorite colors from your yarn stash. Even tiny lengths of yarn would be enough to add a single stitch of color to a motif, bringing it alive and creating just the right color balance.

All the motifs in this book are knitted in stockinette (stocking) stitch using the Intarsia technique and no fancy stitch work is involved—if you can knit and purl, you can create Intarsia motifs.

Inspired by vintage woolen nursery knits and toys, traditional Scandinavian folk art, patterned and printed dress fabrics, and buttons and books, these motifs have all been knitted in a pure Shetland wool 4-ply yarn. This yarn is available in more than 80 different shades—and with some of the dye recipes having remained unchanged for decades, the yarn is perfect for producing authentically charming children's and babies' knits.

Using Colors

Choosing colors to knit with is usually a very personal decision but deciding how to combine and proportion these colors successfully can become an informed choice.

Colors affect each other. On the positive side, they can blend in tonally, support and complement or enhance and balance. On the negative side, they can clash or reduce impact. To understand how color works you can study color theory books, but just as importantly you can experiment directly with knitting yarns, learning from your own experiences and creating your own personal preferences. Gather together a group of favorite colors and start knitting, record successful combinations and keep a scrapbook of found objects, magazine cuttings, or old postcards for color reference and inspiration.

I prefer to work with a color palette that includes grays and browns, slightly muted shades of reds, pinks, oranges, and yellows, avoiding too many pastels.

Combining Colors

For visual impact and ease of knitting the number of colors used for these motifs have been kept to a minimum. There will usually be no more than three or four including the background, and any extra color can be embroidered afterward as highlights.

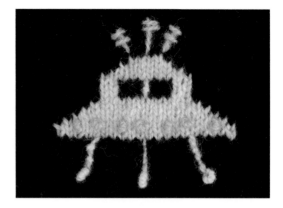

Visually the motif needs to be prominent on the garment and the colors used must not look either too harsh or too washed out against the background color.

When choosing color schemes and tonal color combinations for motifs you can use the following groups as guides to help you: dark backgrounds with lighter colors, light backgrounds with darker colors and tonal colors.

1. A dark background with a lighter color for the motif, can be one of the simplest and most successful ways of combining just two main colors. Often the motif will appear more prominent.

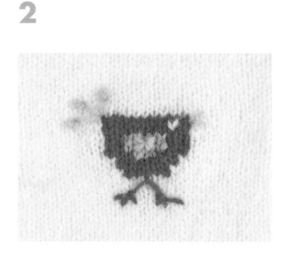

2. A light background with a darker color for the motif is equally as successful. A lighter background usually enables a greater use of colors as other colors and tones will show up easily.

3. Tones of the same color can work very well for the background and the main color. Equally, using compatible tones of color can make motifs appear more complex and interesting.

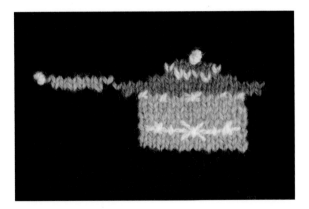

Colored Borders

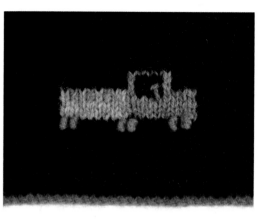

If you add colored borders or stripes, it will help to highlight and emphasize a motif, creating a more unified knitted garment. The colors used for the motif can be incorporated into the garment either in isolation as a single row of highlight color or combined together as stripes or larger colored borders.

Small motifs such as the Truck (page 85), Little Garden Flowers (page 75), and the Little Squeaks (page 31) would benefit from a single highlighting stripe of color.

The Robot (page 86), Anil the Elephant (page 23), and the Man in the Moon (page 55) would work well with a combination of colorful stripes.

The Reindeer (page 45), Pear (page 67), and the Sun (page 54) would look good with a simple, bright, single-colored border, picking up one of the motif colors, to emphasize their graphic shape.

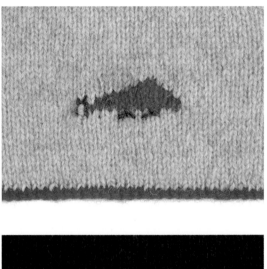

Yarn Choices

The motifs in this book should work well knitted with any choice of yarn in either wool, silk, cotton, or linen. So long as the yarn weights in the motif and the knitted background are the same, motifs can be knitted with any chosen weight of yarn.

It is, in my opinion, much easier to knit Intarsia with a pure wool yarn as it is more forgiving and more stretchy than other yarns and a pure wool can be washed before wearing to fluff up and "felt" the knitting slightly. Different yarn weights will affect the scale of the motif so do consider carefully which motif you want to knit with which yarn.

In this book, I have used a pure wool 4-ply yarn for all the motifs, as it provides the perfect scale for small projects, such as babies' or little children's garments. In the photographs (right) and all the five main sections, the motifs appear the same size as the original knitting. If you use thicker yarn, the motif will increase in scale accordingly. The images (right) show the same motif knitted in 4-ply (top), double knitting (center), and chunky (bottom).

If you are knitting a large item, such as a blanket, it may be worth your while to use a thicker yarn, but do be aware that the motifs will also be larger, too, and take this into account when planning your design.

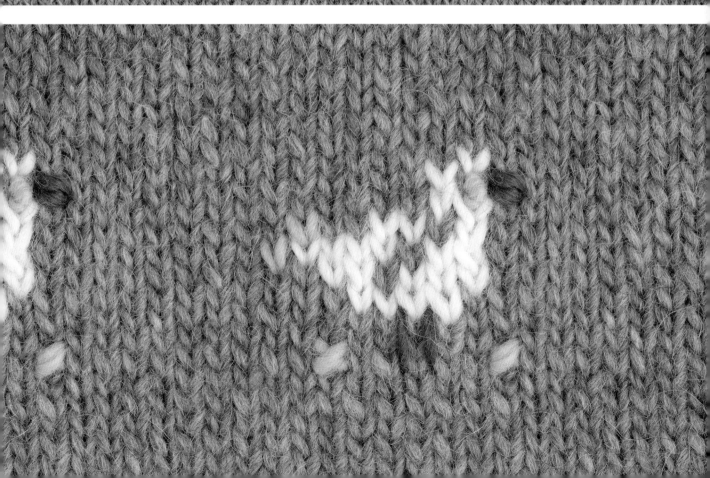

Placement and Sizing

The same motif can be successfully used on a variety of different-sized garments, but its impact and scale will vary. For example, the Little Folk Heart and Flowers (page 47) is the perfect size when using 4-ply yarn for a single motif on a toddler's top. Combined with a larger motif, like the Dancing Folk Figures (page 38), it works well on an older child's pinafore.

When placing motifs you will need to consider that the weight of yarn you use will affect the scale of the motif—how much impact the motif will have. Is it too large or small for a garment? How will the garment hang and fold when being worn? How much wear and tear will the area with the motif receive in this position?

Once you have decided which motif or combination of motifs you want to use and where you want them, you will need to calculate how to place them exactly within your pattern. You could work directly onto graph paper, drawing up the shape of the garment and then drawing in the motif, stating exactly where you want it, knitting directly from this chart. Alternatively, calculate the number of stitches and rows needed for the motif or motifs and write the pattern instructions down stating exactly where it will be incorporated.

If you want to use several motifs equally spaced around a sweater you will need to count the number of stitches there are in the motif and then calculate how many stitches you want in between them. If you are working from a knitting pattern with a set number of stitches you will be restricted to that number and will have to accommodate the motifs as best as you can. However, if you make up your own patterns, you will be able to work out exactly what you need to make the motifs work well on the pattern.

Combining Motifs

Any of the motifs in this book can make continuous all-over patterns. For a successful choice of motifs, you need to consider the scale and subject of the motifs, how well the motifs sit together and also the best colors to use.

You can experiment with combinations by photocopying the black and white motif charts at the end of each chapter and placing them in groups. Or you could draw motifs directly onto a photocopied piece of the special chart paper on pages 108–109.

The borders (right, top to bottom), show combinations of motifs as follows:

Little Garden Flowers (page 75)
Hearts (page 43)
Butterflies (page 57)

Chickadee (page 28)
Star (page 44)

Garden Flowers (page 72)
Anil the Elephant (page 23)

Little Folk Heart and Flowers (page 47)
Little Birds (page 46)

Kettles (page 58)
Pears (page 67)

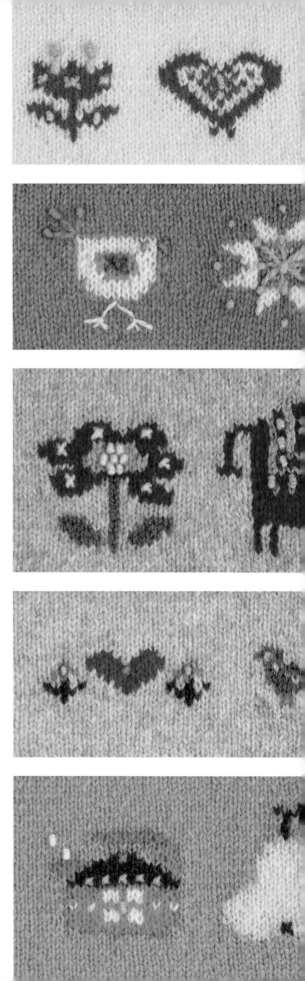

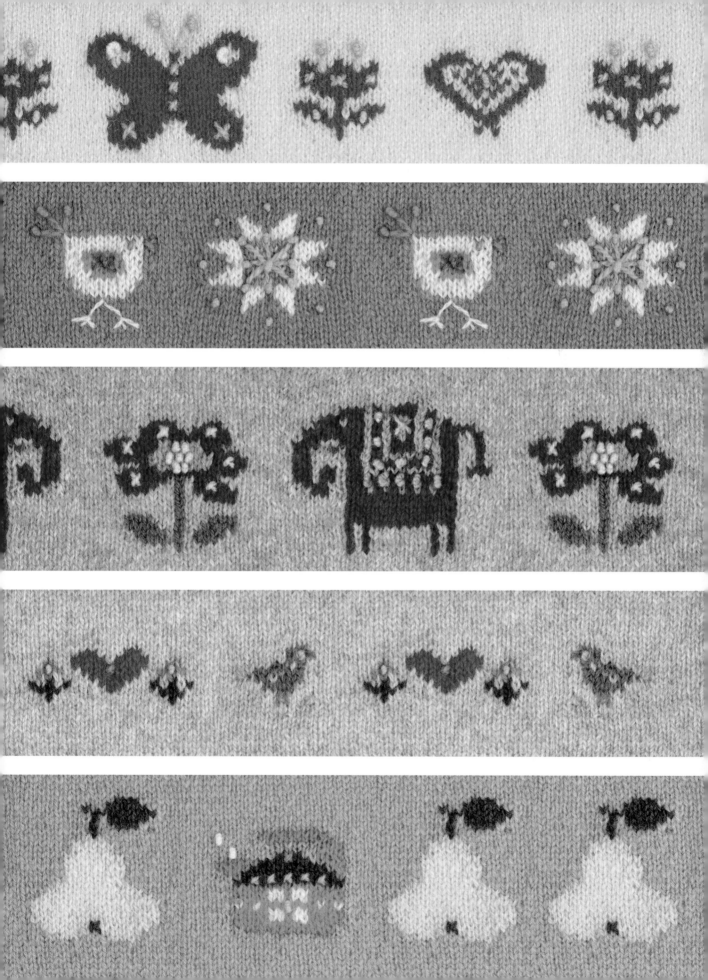

Animals and Birds

Lars the Lion

With his great mane created from simple straight stitches and his little bottlebrush tail, made from another few straight stitches, this happy lion is the pride of the pack. He looks good on his own or placed in matching pairs—set tail to tail. Flip the chart to work the motif in alternating directions.

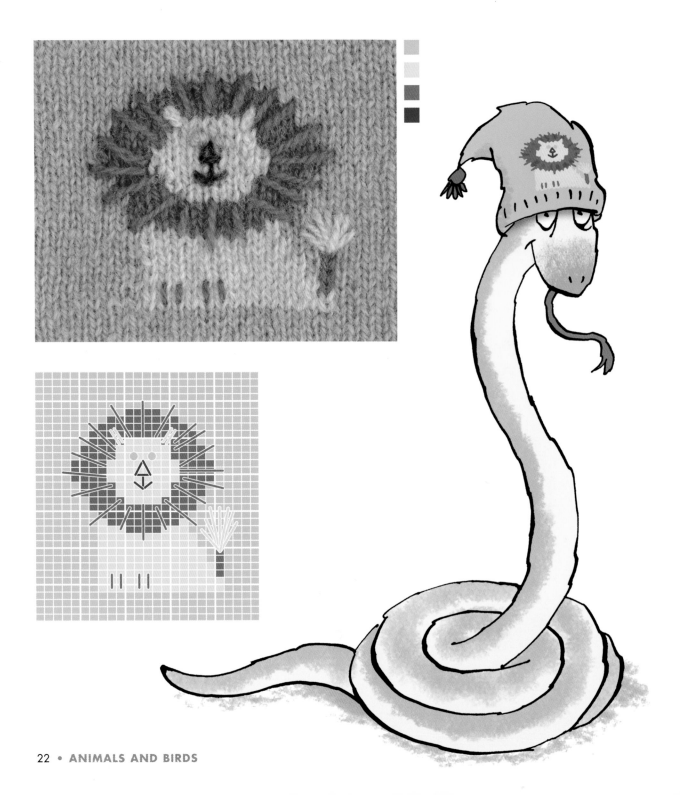

Anil the Elephant

Anil is looking handsome and is in a party mood as he is wearing his wonderfully decorated, festive canopy. Simple French knots, a duplicate stitch eye, and a cross stitch are all the embellishment he needs to brighten up any dress, pullover, or pocket. Anil makes the perfect decoration for a special party bag.

DESIGN IDEAS

If you want a matching pair of elephants facing each other on your design, then simply photocopy the chart and flip it over to get a reverse image. Anil would look great, too, if you change the color order for each elephant.

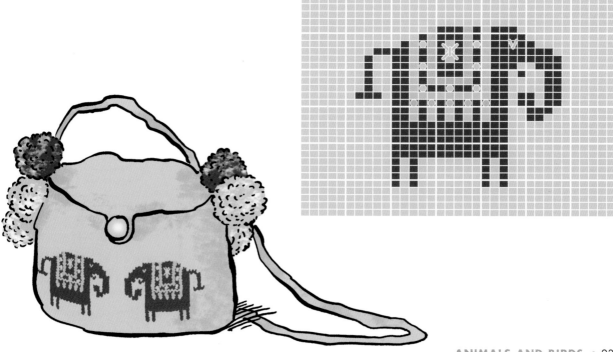

Flossie and Pod Rabbits

These two sweet little rabbits make delightful individual motifs for a child's bib, hat, or scarf but look equally good when used together. You can mix the colors in the row, but take care that they show up equally well against the background color. A few simple embroidery stitches create the rabbits' faces and paws.

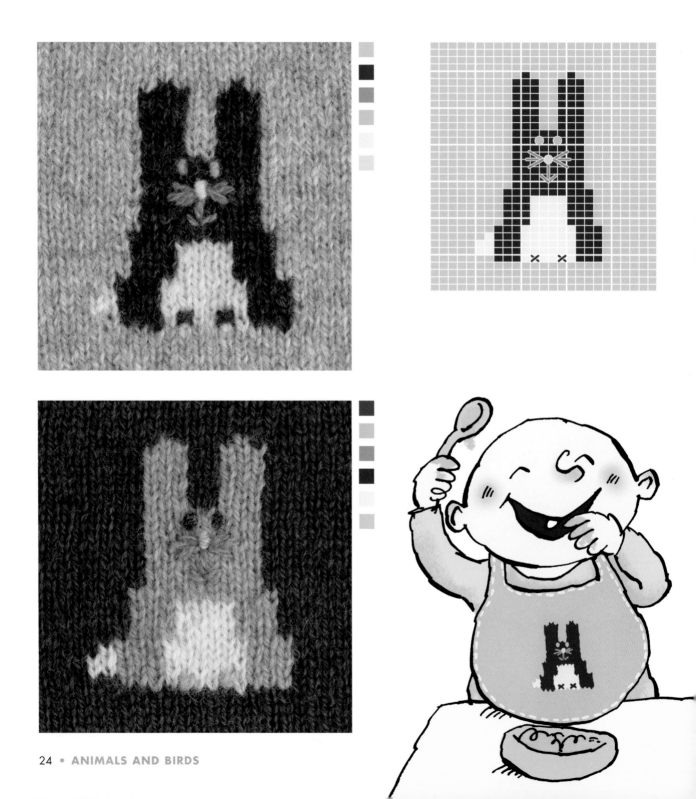

Boris the Dog

Dogs are always popular and with his nonchalant attitude this spotty hound is no exception. His mouth is a single embroidery stitch and his eye and paws are duplicate stitches. You could simplify knitting Boris the Dog by using duplicate stitches for his collar and even his spots.

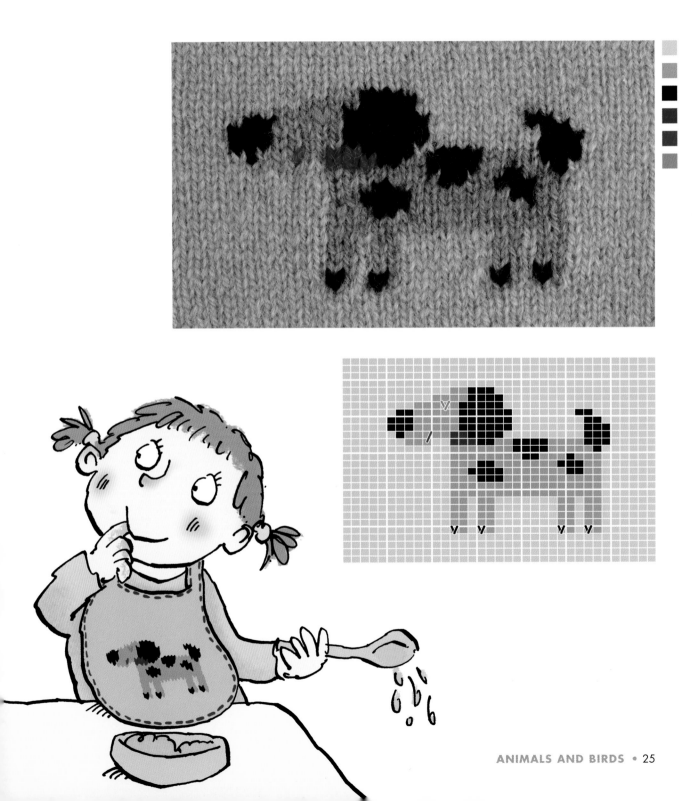

Elgar Owl

Elgar is a cheerful little owl whose brightly embroidered chest and wings make him a perfect motif for a cozy winter hat or at each end of a warm scarf. Elgar Owl would also look great on the pockets of a winter coat or repeated in a row as a border for a wooly blanket.

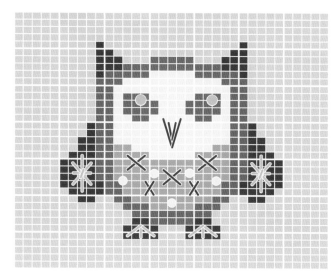

TECHNIQUE TIPS

Minimize the number of yarn ends by using a long enough length of yarn to complete all the embroidery in each color in one go.

Hansel and Lotta Hedgehogs

Happy hedgehogs Hansel and Lotta would look very sweet as decoration for a cozy winter sweater or blanket, especially if they were combined with the Elgar Owl motif (opposite) and the Toadstool motif (page 41). They also make a great border if used on their own, as shown on the little bag below.

DESIGN IDEAS

If you want to make the hedgehog's spines longer, you could use bullion knots (page 103), in which the yarn is twisted many more times around the needle, in a little curl, instead of the French knots I have used here. You could also make these in lots of different colors.

Chickadee

Chickadee is a sweet, perky little bird who will look good on smaller items such as baby hats and jackets. Chickadee's tail feathers are long straight stitches finished with French knots, her wing markings have a little cross stitch with another French knot in the center, and her beak, feet, and legs are straight stitches and her eye is a duplicate stitch.

Kossoff the Whale

This big, bold whale is easy to knit in one color and, with the addition of just a few embroidery stitches, he is quickly finished and ready to wear. Kossoff would look great in a school of whales, swimming around the hem of a skirt or sweater and would look equally good knitted in bright blue on a white background.

DESIGN IDEAS

If you want a school of whales swimming along a border you can have them facing each other in matching pairs by simply photocopying the black and white Whale chart (page 34) in reverse.

Alternatively, photocopy and use the special graph paper provided (pages 108–109) and draw the Whale in reverse.

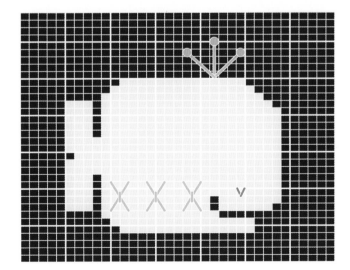

Monette Mouse and the Little Squeaks

These cute little mice make delightful motifs for small items like purses or pockets, or as an individual motif on a scarf just like the one the cat is wearing below. Create alternating rows of Little Squeaks and Monette Mouse for a super mousie garment. All the mice have simple straight stitches for their tails and whiskers and a French knot for their noses.

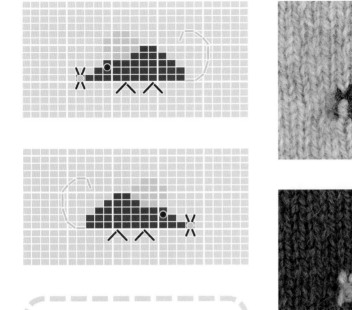

DESIGN IDEAS

Try repeating the Little Squeaks in rows, alternating the direction they are running in, as shown on the scarf that the cat is wearing below.

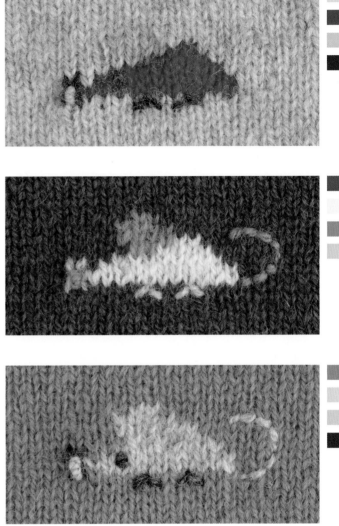

The Big Pughs and the Ginger Toms

The Big Pughs are happy cats, and they will brighten up the simplest of sweaters or hats. They look great on their own decorating a pair of pockets, or placed either side of a baby's jacket. The Ginger Toms make an excellent border, as you can see below, and would also look very sweet, facing each other on each front of a toddler's cardigan.

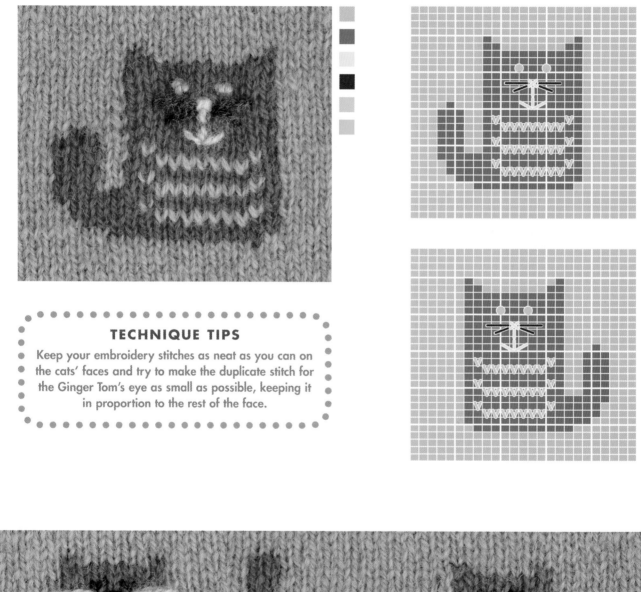

TECHNIQUE TIPS

Keep your embroidery stitches as neat as you can on the cats' faces and try to make the duplicate stitch for the Ginger Tom's eye as small as possible, keeping it in proportion to the rest of the face.

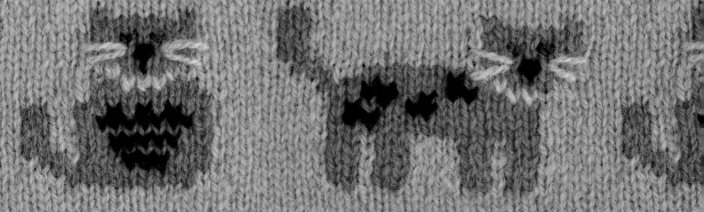

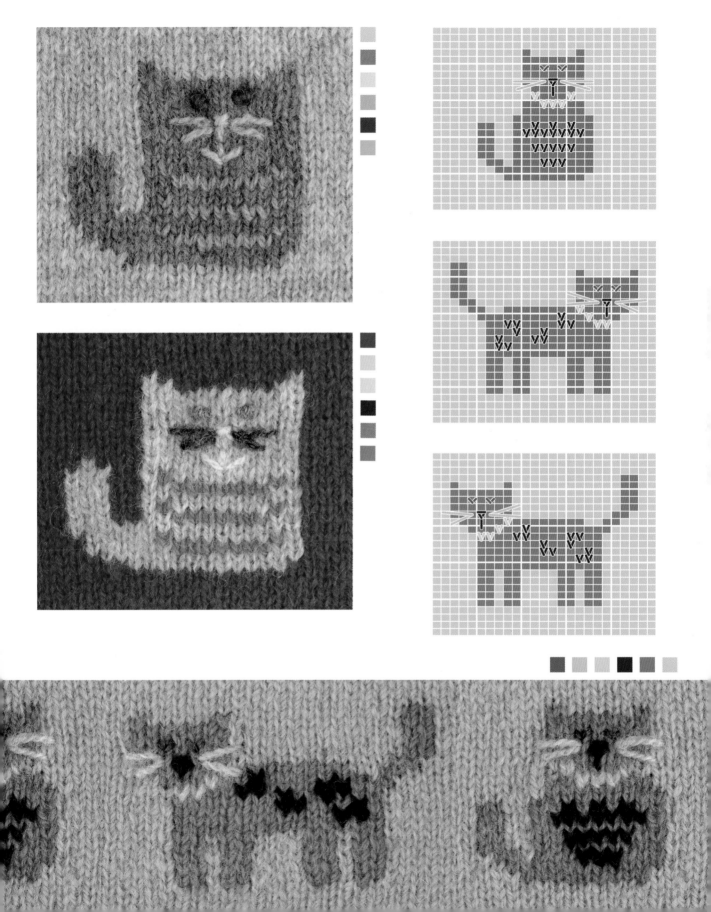

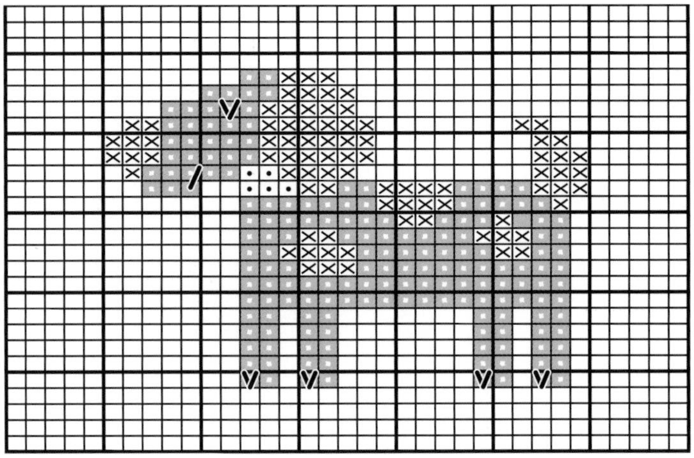

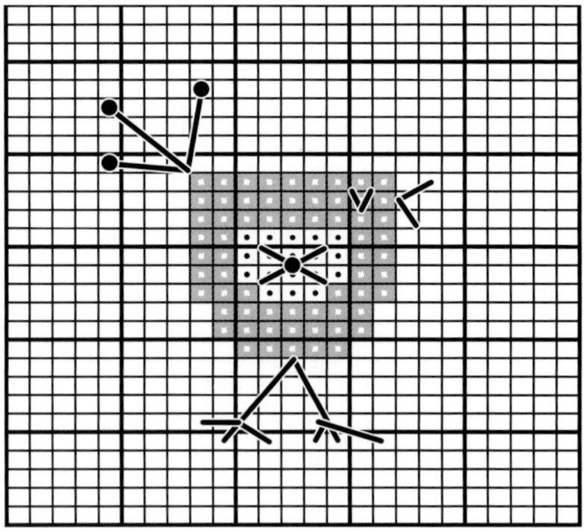

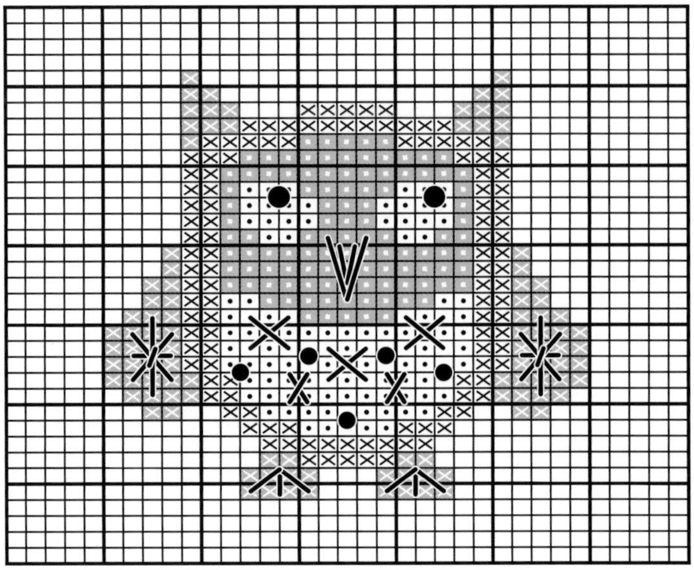

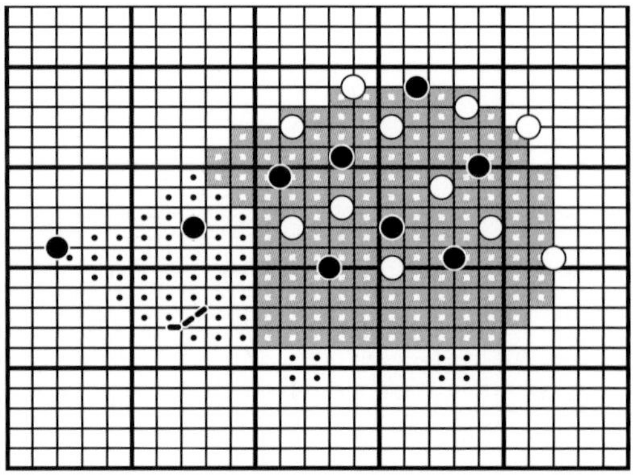

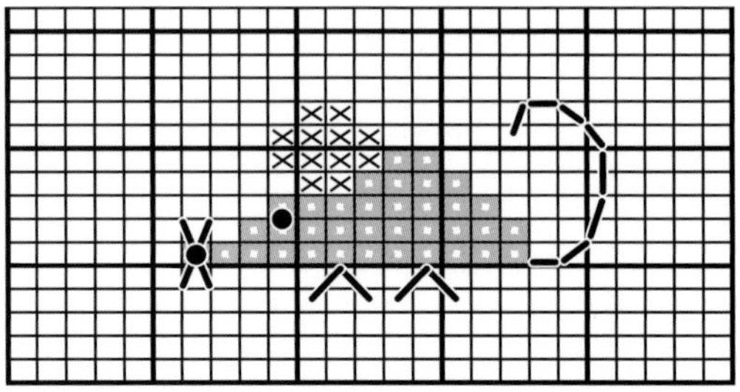

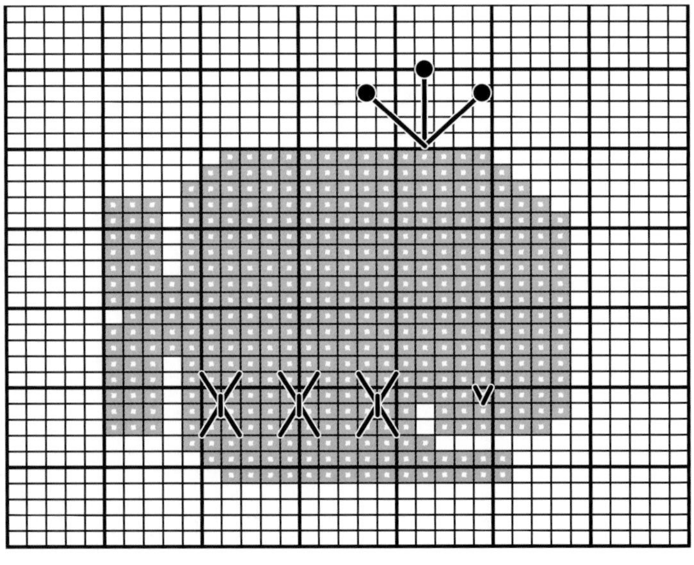

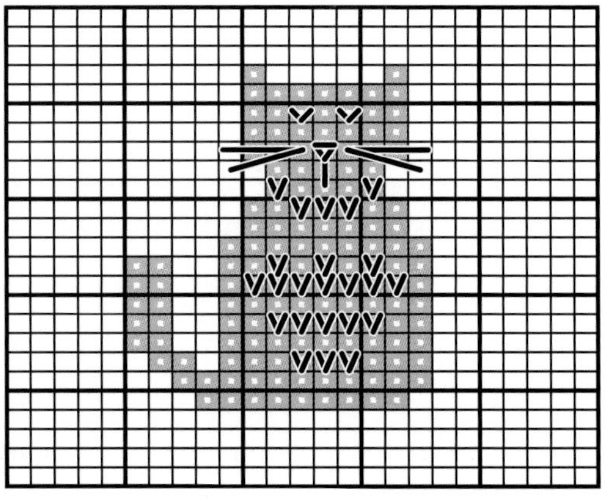

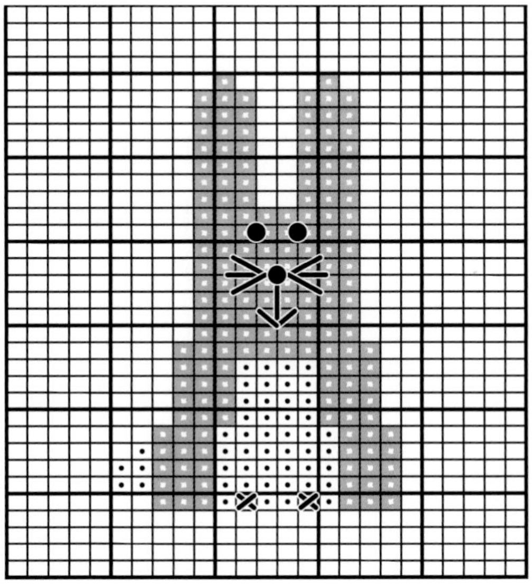
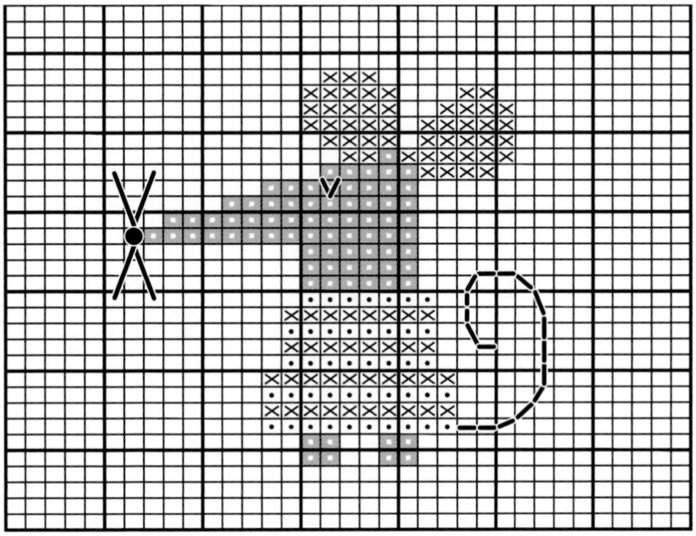
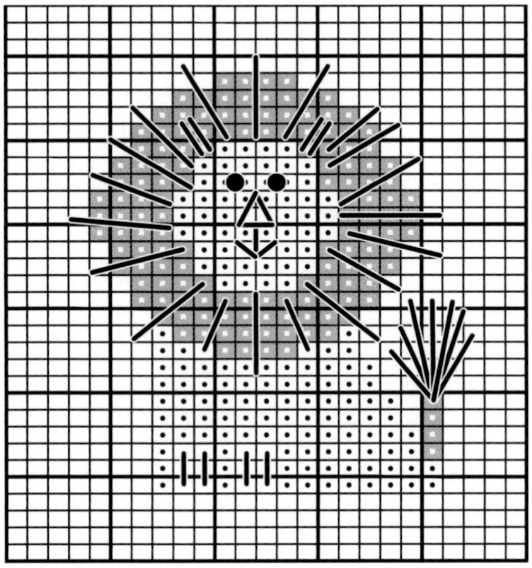
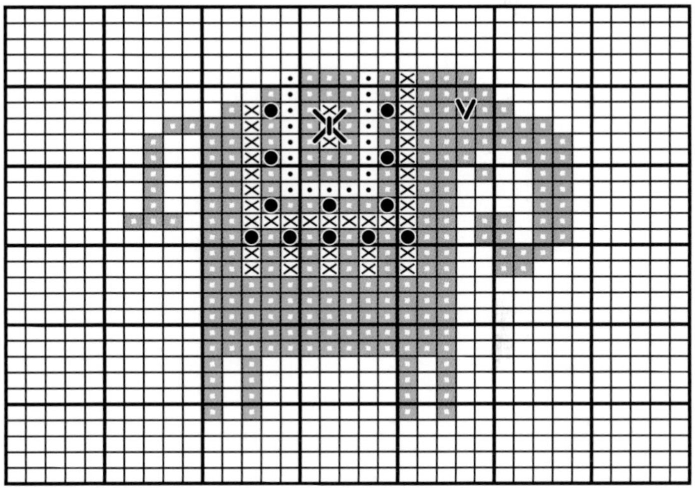
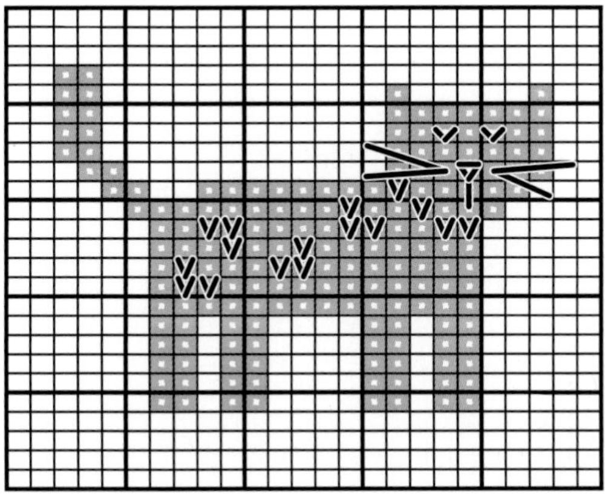
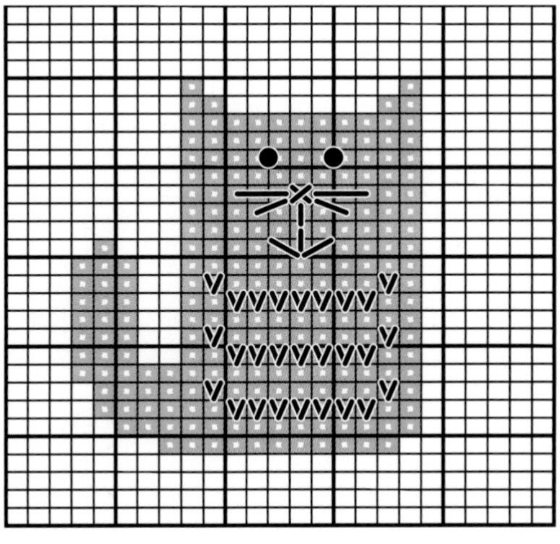

Traditional Folk

Dancing Folk Figures

Inspired by the little men and women motifs used in traditional Norwegian knitwear, these attractive little figures look fun used together with joined hands dancing around the hem of a dress, just like the ones these little girls are wearing. The Dancing Folk Figures combine perfectly with the Little Folk Heart and Flowers motif (page 47).

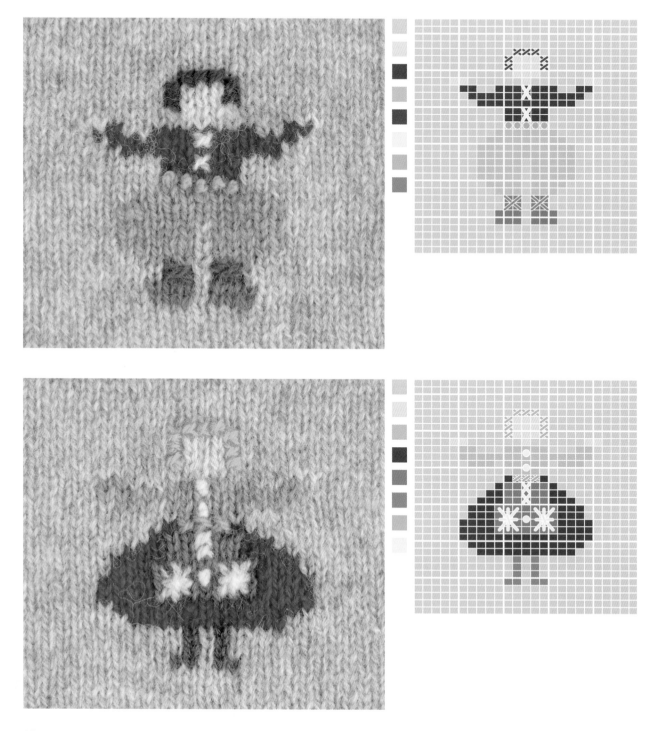

DESIGN IDEAS

Use these Dancing Folk Figures as single motifs on
patchwork squares to make a bright and colorful folk
blanket. Try alternating the squares with other Folk
designs such as the Hearts (page 43) and Star (page 44)
or with simple geometrics (page 104).

Big Folk Bird

A piece of beautiful Swedish lace work was the inspiration for this Big Folk Bird. Easily knitted in just one color with simple bright embroidery stitches for decoration, the Big Folk Bird looks very festive in red and white, making it an ideal embellishment for a winter hat and coat or even a decoration in itself to hang.

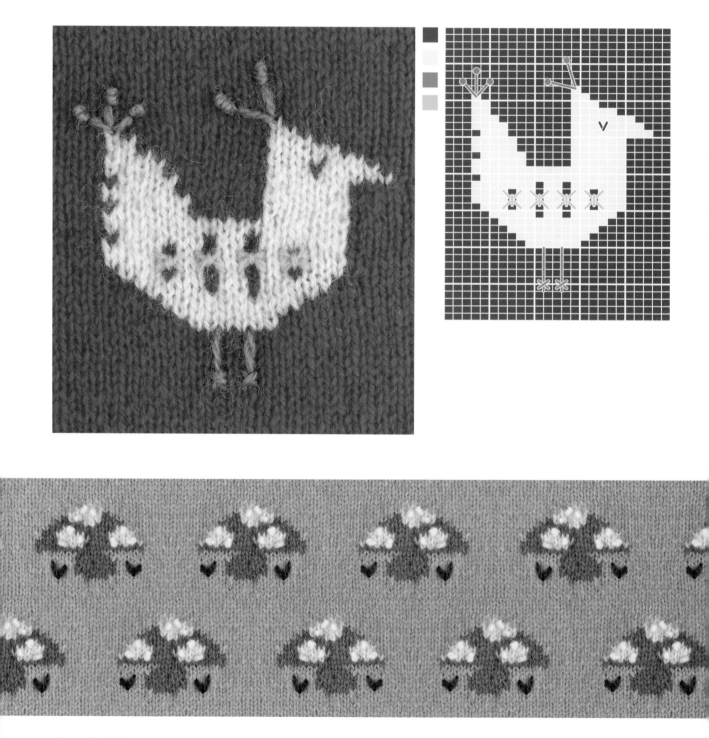

Toadstool

This bright little Toadstool with its textured embroidery stitches would look very cute as a single motif on a baby's vest or hat. Try repeating and flipping the toadstools, as shown in the charts and border below, to make a fabulous edging for a cozy baby's blanket or a bag for woodland walks.

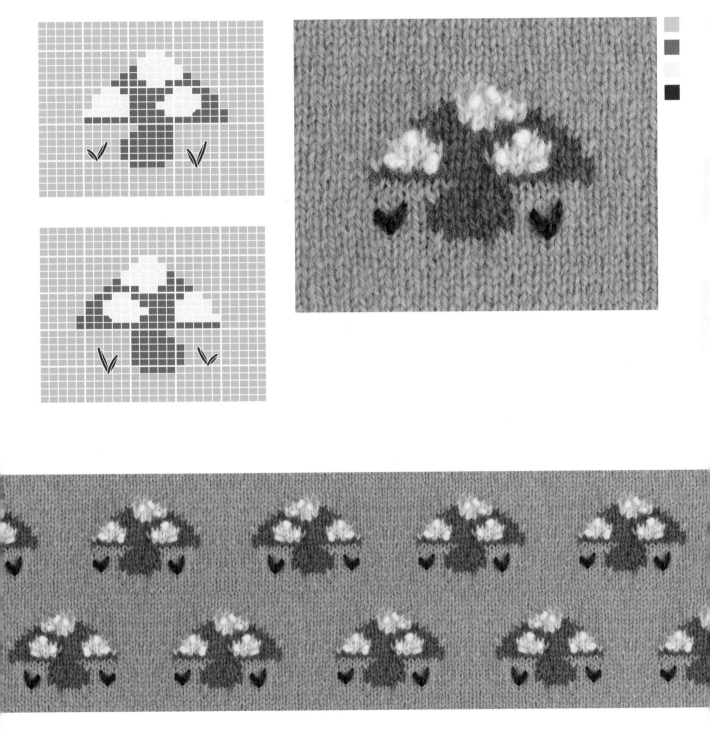

Folk Girls

These little Folk Girls were inspired by the Scandinavian figures that can be found on both vintage and modern children's knitwear. With the addition of a little embroidery in a contrasting color, the Folk Girls would be just right to brighten up a pocket on a dress or could be placed in a repeat pattern for a stylish yoke on a girl's sweater.

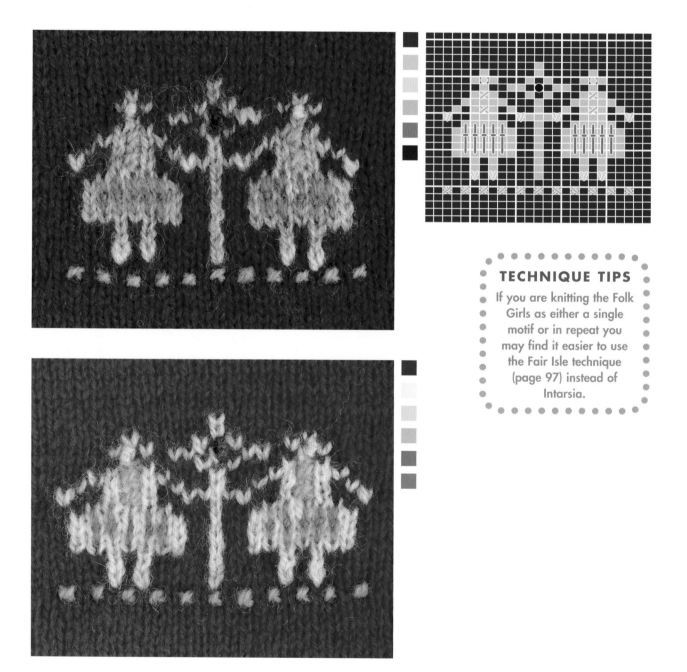

TECHNIQUE TIPS

If you are knitting the Folk Girls as either a single motif or in repeat you may find it easier to use the Fair Isle technique (page 97) instead of Intarsia.

Hearts

These lovely traditional Hearts were inspired by a pair of beautifully embroidered Swedish mittens and will look sweet on any child's or baby's garment. They are easily knitted in just one color with a single bullion knot as decoration. You may find it easier to use the Fair Isle technique to knit the patterned center of the heart.

Star

Festive, bright, and beautiful, this Star looks great used as a single motif on a wooly winter hat just like the one the little boy is wearing. The Star motif would also look stunning as an all-over pattern for a blanket or cushion, especially if you used lots of different colors for the embroidery.

Reindeer

Knitted Reindeer motifs are synonymous with traditional Scandinavian ski wear and this perky little Reindeer would make a wonderful patterned yoke for a child's wooly winter sweater, like the one the little boy is wearing below. Simple embroidered cross stitches and a single star stitch create a traditional folk look and feel.

DESIGN IDEAS

If repeated, this Reindeer motif makes a wonderful border. Try using different colored embroidery for each Reindeer to make the border especially beautiful.

Little Birds

Inspired by exquisitely embroidered, painted, and knitted motifs found in traditional Scandinavian folk art, these dainty Little Birds are the perfect motifs to decorate the smallest and most delicate of baby knits. A single Little Bird would look very charming on a cap for a newborn baby or on a pair of booties or socks.

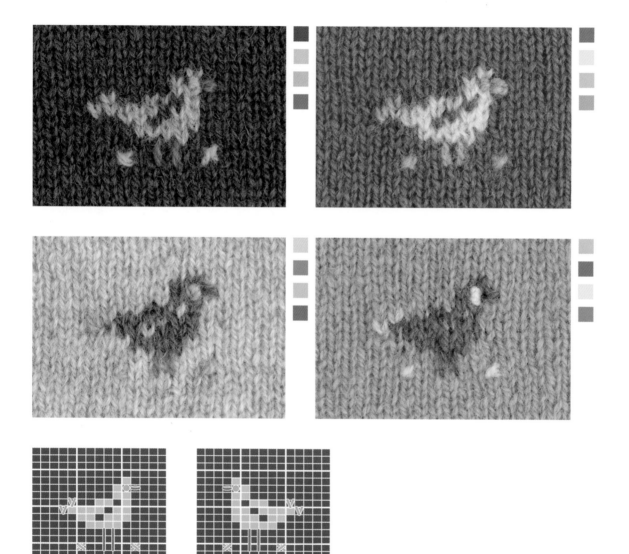

Little Folk Heart and Flowers

Brightly colored Tyrolean folk designs were the inspiration for these versatile Little Folk Heart and Flowers motifs. They look equally lovely used on their own or in groups and repeated in rows. Try combining them with the other traditional Folk motifs like the Dancing Folk Figures (page 38) and the Little Birds (opposite).

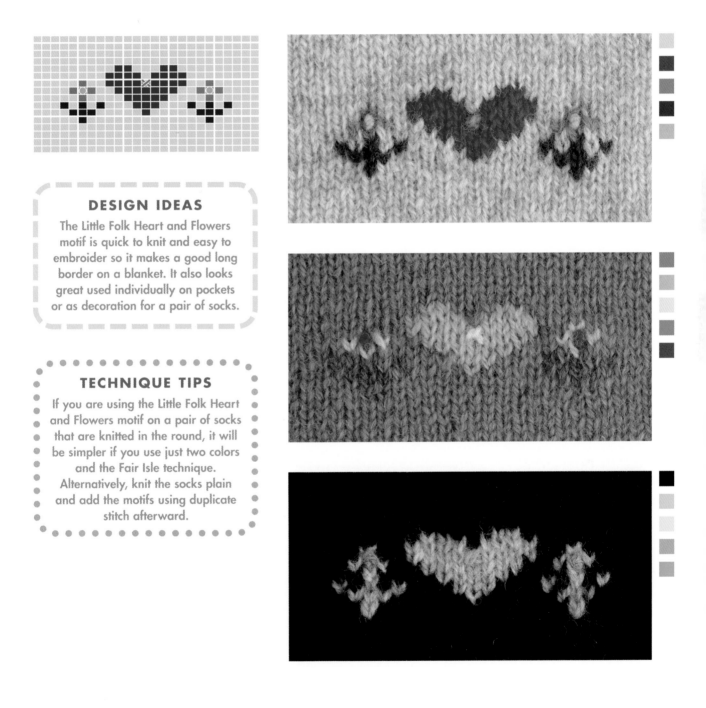

DESIGN IDEAS

The Little Folk Heart and Flowers motif is quick to knit and easy to embroider so it makes a good long border on a blanket. It also looks great used individually on pockets or as decoration for a pair of socks.

TECHNIQUE TIPS

If you are using the Little Folk Heart and Flowers motif on a pair of socks that are knitted in the round, it will be simpler if you use just two colors and the Fair Isle technique. Alternatively, knit the socks plain and add the motifs using duplicate stitch afterward.

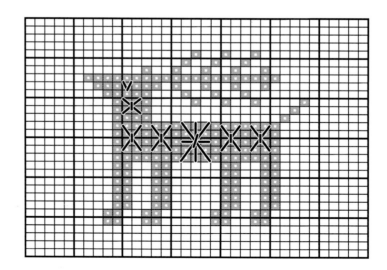

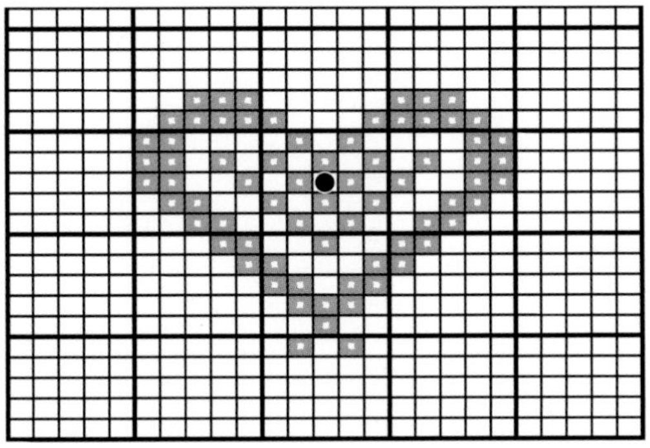
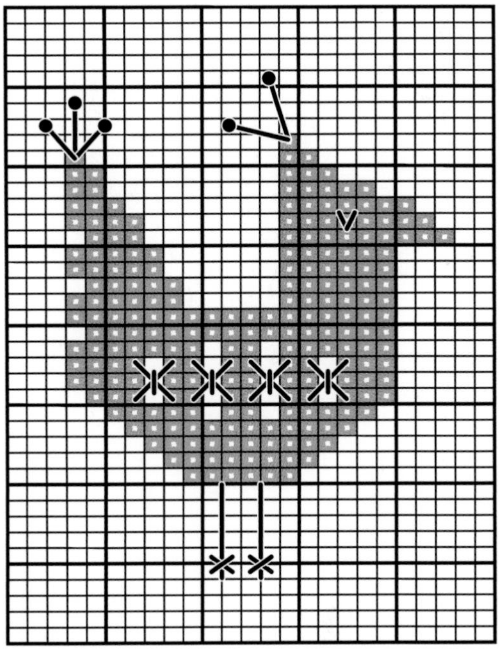
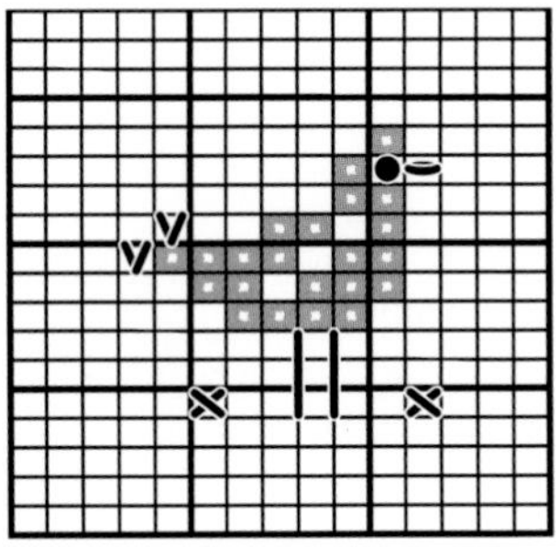
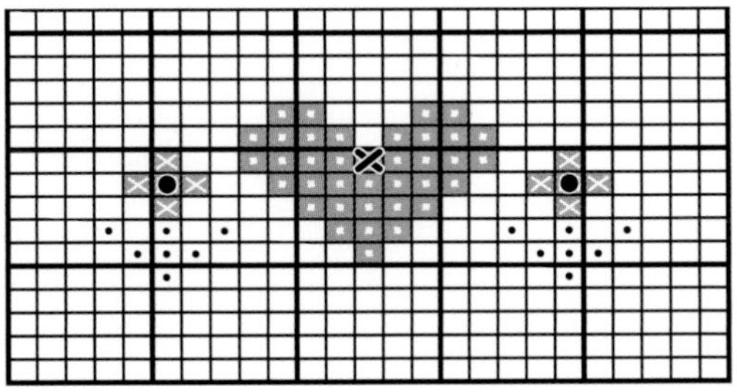
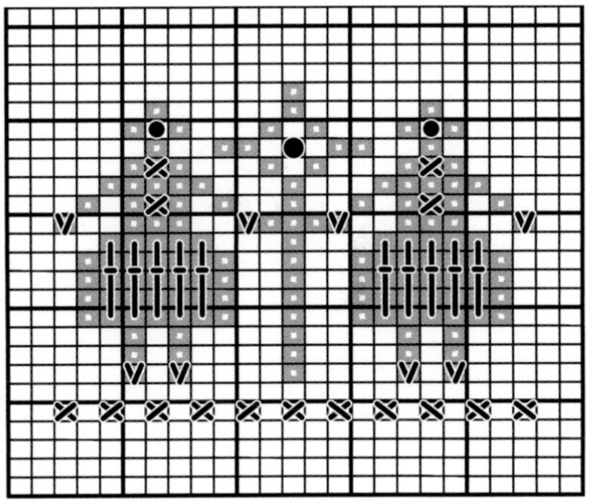

House

Neat and bright, this little House would look great on any nursery knits. Use simple long straight stitches to make the window panes and French knots for the door handle and chimney smoke. Try repeating the House motif in a row using lots of different colors to make a whole street!

Tree

This stylized Tree is simply knitted in just two colors and uses French knots to make the apples and duplicate stitches to make the leaves. Combine the Tree motif with the House motif, as shown below, to make a stunning border for a nursery blanket or cushion. Alternatively, you could knit the Tree in golden brown tones for a Fall-themed knit!

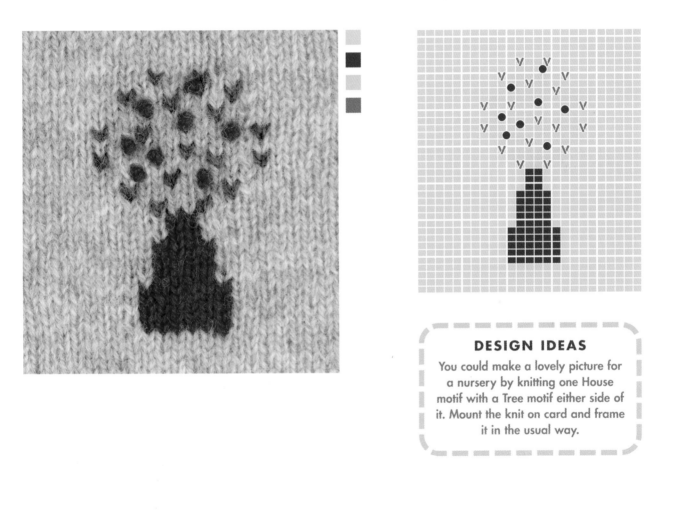

DESIGN IDEAS

You could make a lovely picture for a nursery by knitting one House motif with a Tree motif either side of it. Mount the knit on card and frame it in the usual way.

Sun

Here comes the sunshine! This golden, happy little Sun, with his simple embroidered face, will brighten up any child's or baby's garment or even a hot-water bottle cover! Use the Sun on his own or combine him with other motifs like the Man in the Moon (opposite), Butterflies (page 57), House (page 52), and Clouds (pages 60–61).

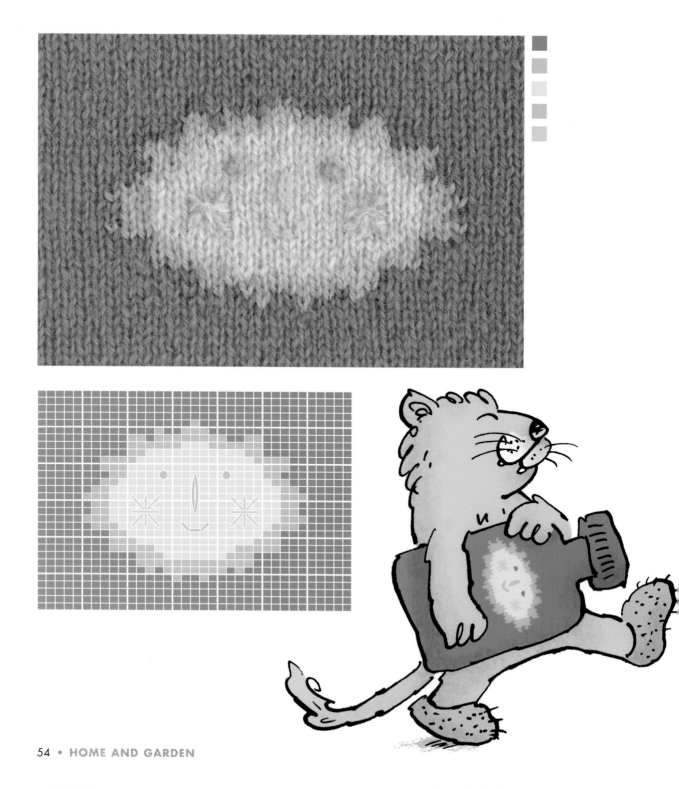

Man in the Moon

Bedtime nursery knits will not be complete unless they have a sleepy Man in the Moon as decoration. The Man in the Moon looks very handsome, bright, and luminous on the inky blue background used for this little boy's robe. He would also look great on socks and slippers, especially if combined with Elgar Owl (page 26).

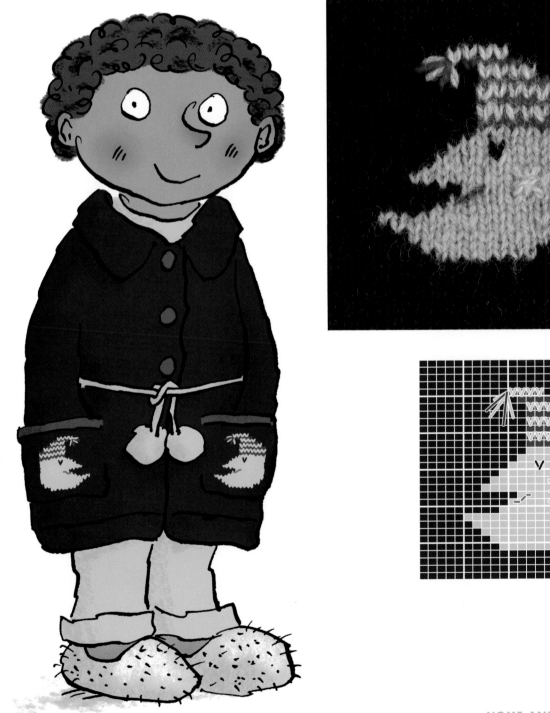

Bug

This big, bad Bug definitely has attitude! He will, however, look really striking marching around the border of sweaters, bags, blankets, or little dresses. Very simple embroidery stitches are all that is needed to create his mischievous character with its very determined march.

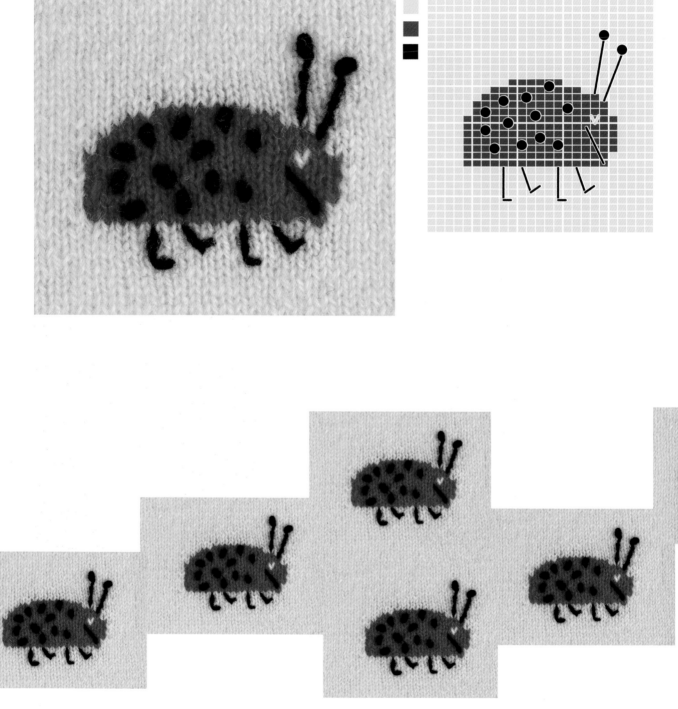

Butterflies

Bold and beautiful, these big Butterflies make the perfect square for a patchwork blanket. You could alternate brightly colored ones with softer toned ones for a pretty pram or crib blanket. Or simply stitch two Butterfly squares together and fill with dried lavender for a scented sachet for a drawer.

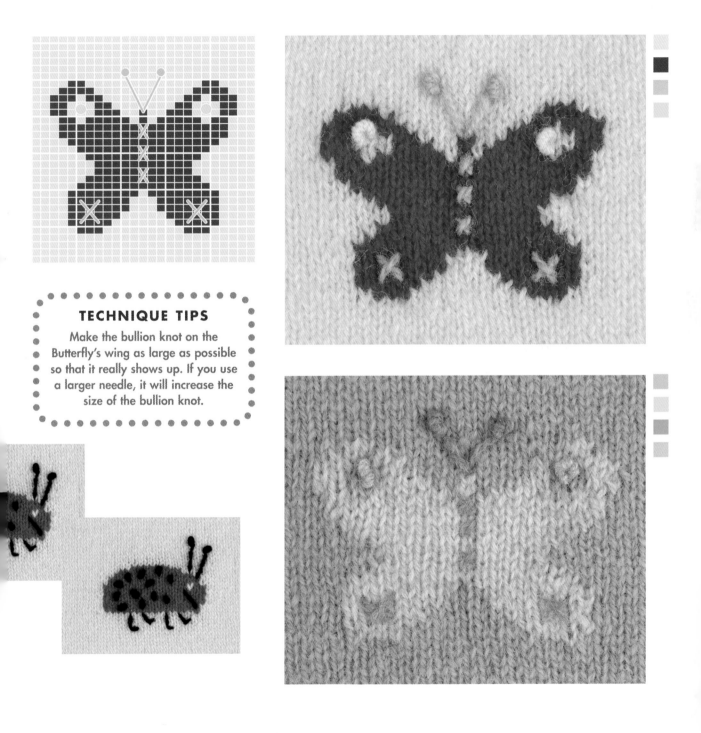

TECHNIQUE TIPS

Make the bullion knot on the Butterfly's wing as large as possible so that it really shows up. If you use a larger needle, it will increase the size of the bullion knot.

Kettles

If you put the Kettle motif on the pocket of a child's knitted top or sweater, it will instantly make it more fun to wear. It would also be just right, too, for a baby's bib, a picnic blanket, or even a little egg cozy. With only tiny little cross stitches and several French knots as decoration the Kettles are quick to knit from start to finish.

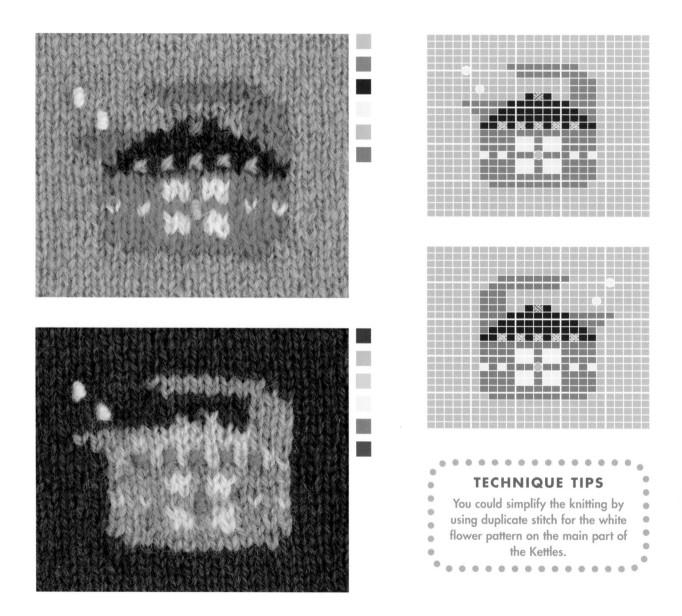

TECHNIQUE TIPS

You could simplify the knitting by using duplicate stitch for the white flower pattern on the main part of the Kettles.

Saucepans

Inspired by wonderful children's book illustrations from the 1960s, these quirky, brightly colored and patterned Saucepans make ideal motifs for babies' bibs. The Saucepans are easily knitted in two colors and the patterns are embroidered using French knots, cross stitches, long straight stitches, and duplicate stitch.

DESIGN IDEAS

Everyday objects like the Saucepans and Kettles make fun motifs to use on a child's cushion for a highchair.

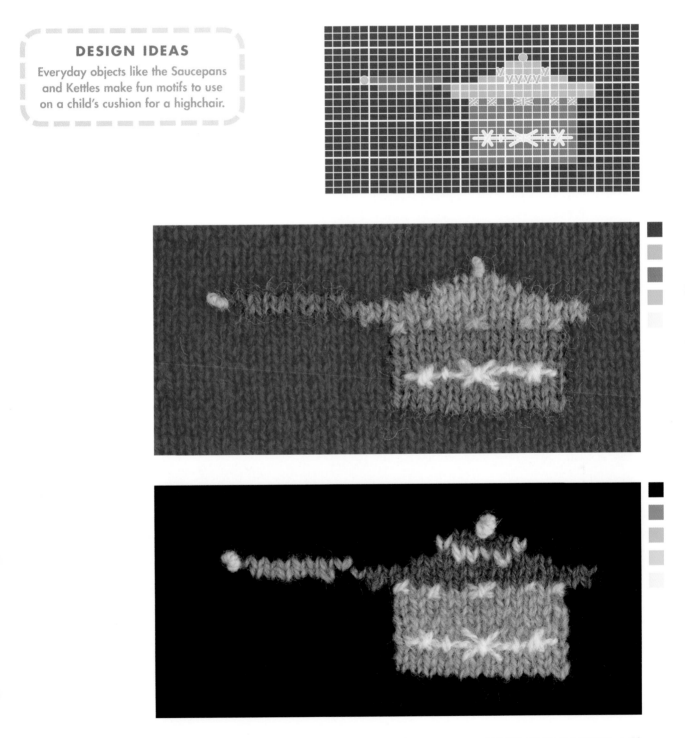

Clouds

Come rain or shine these gorgeous little Clouds make the perfect motif for a child's blanket, bag, or hot-water bottle cover. Alternate the Clouds as shown here or create a more dramatic design using darker blues and soft grays for the background and Cloud.

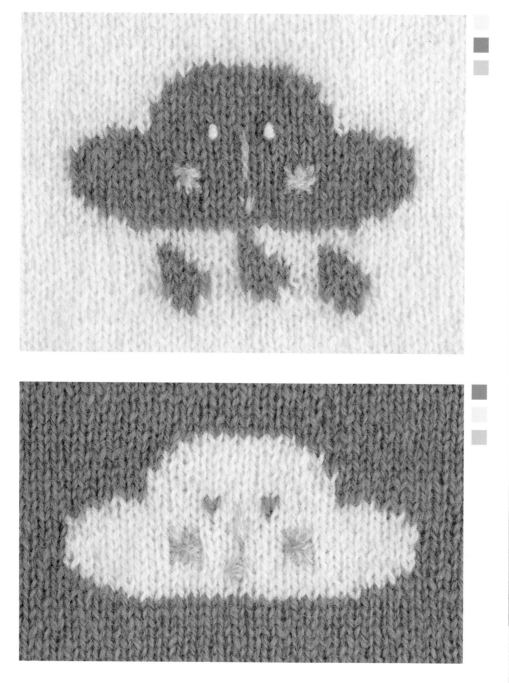

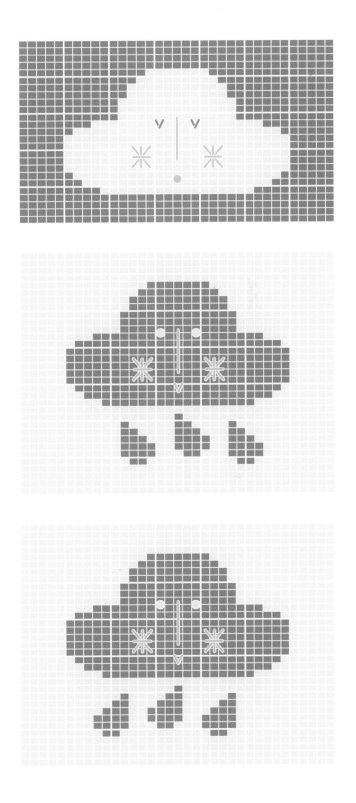

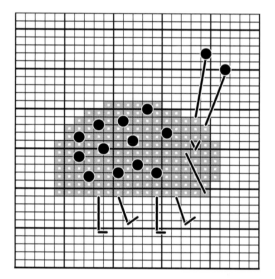

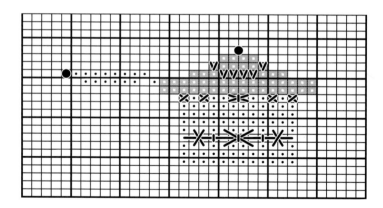

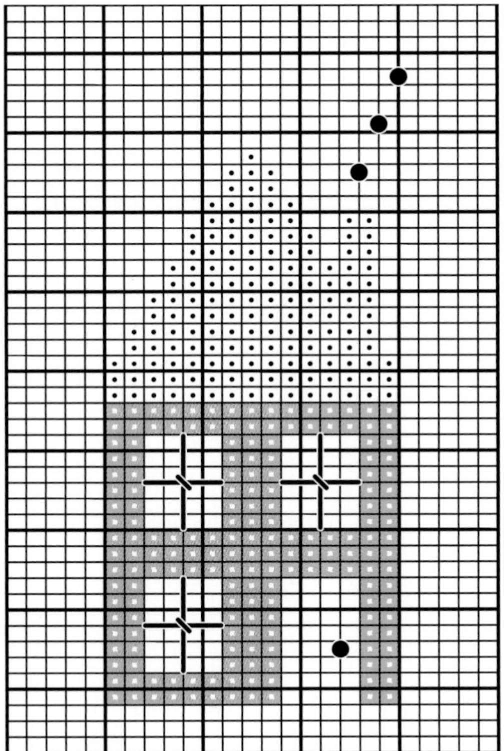

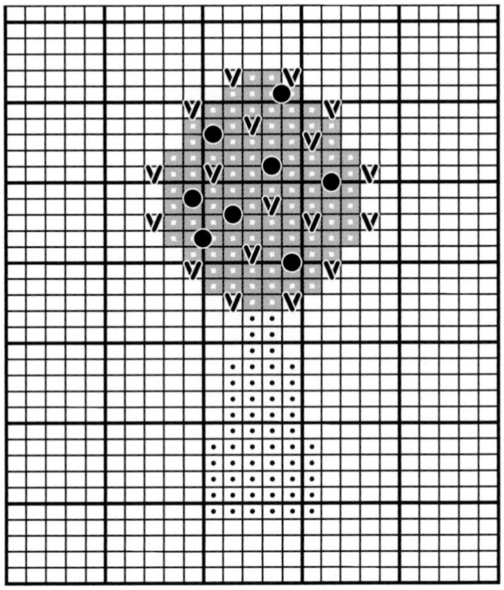

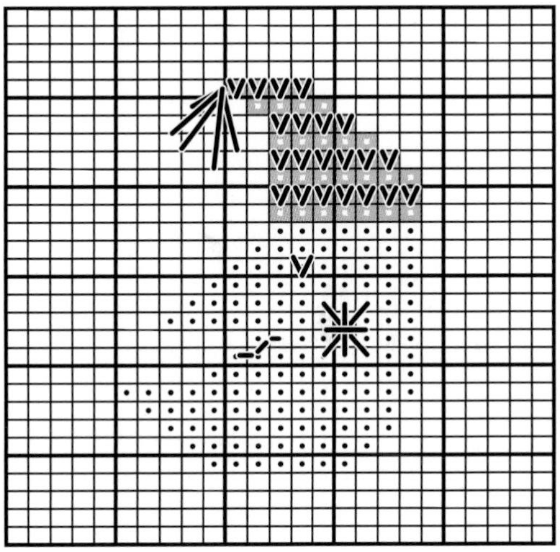

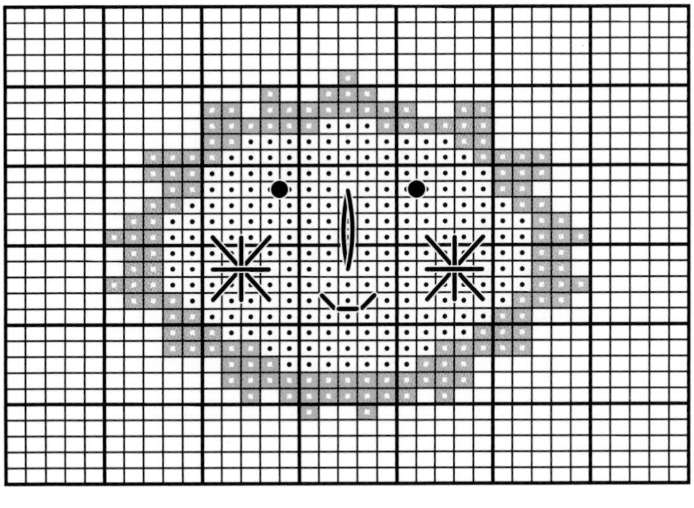

Plants and Flowers

Apples

The Apple is a much-loved motif commonly found in Scandinavian embroideries and is often used to decorate children's and babies' knitwear. Round and rosy, it is easily knitted as a single motif. Or try combining the Apples with other motifs like the Sun (page 54), the Robots (pages 86–87), and the Pears (opposite).

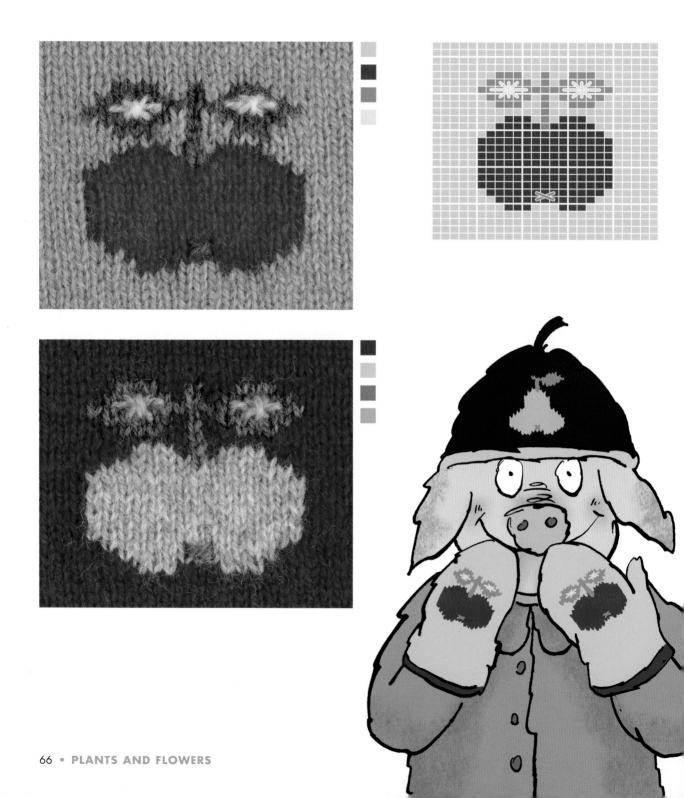

Pears

The Pear is another favorite motif often found on traditional embroideries, and it looks great knitted in either fresh, bold, and bright colors or in darker and more muted shades. With the minimum of embroidery as decoration—just one small cross stitch—these Pears are quickly knitted and finished.

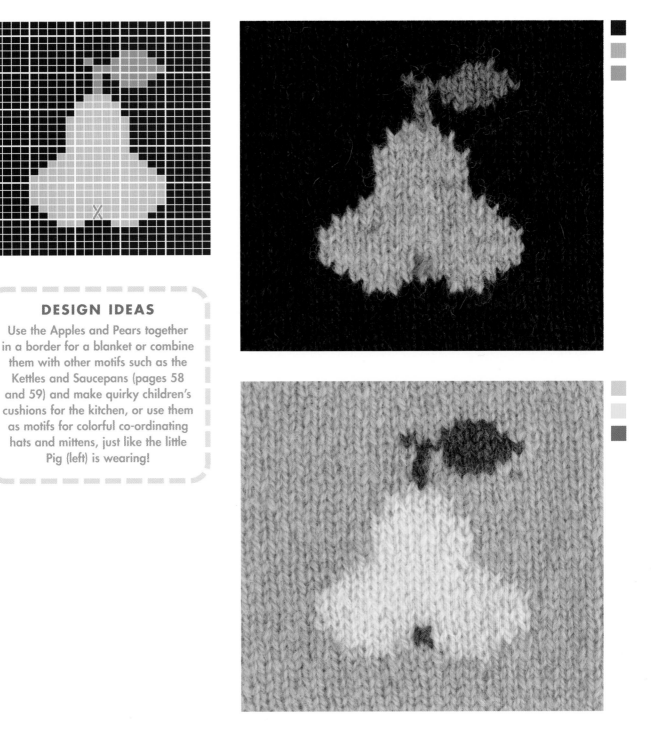

DESIGN IDEAS

Use the Apples and Pears together in a border for a blanket or combine them with other motifs such as the Kettles and Saucepans (pages 58 and 59) and make quirky children's cushions for the kitchen, or use them as motifs for colorful co-ordinating hats and mittens, just like the little Pig (left) is wearing!

Carrot

Most children like crunchy carrots so I am sure they will also love these cute little knitted Carrots. Simple long straight stitches are used for the carrot tops and secured long stitches and cross stitches decorate the carrot itself. The Carrot motif would be fun to combine with Flossie and Pod Rabbits (page 24).

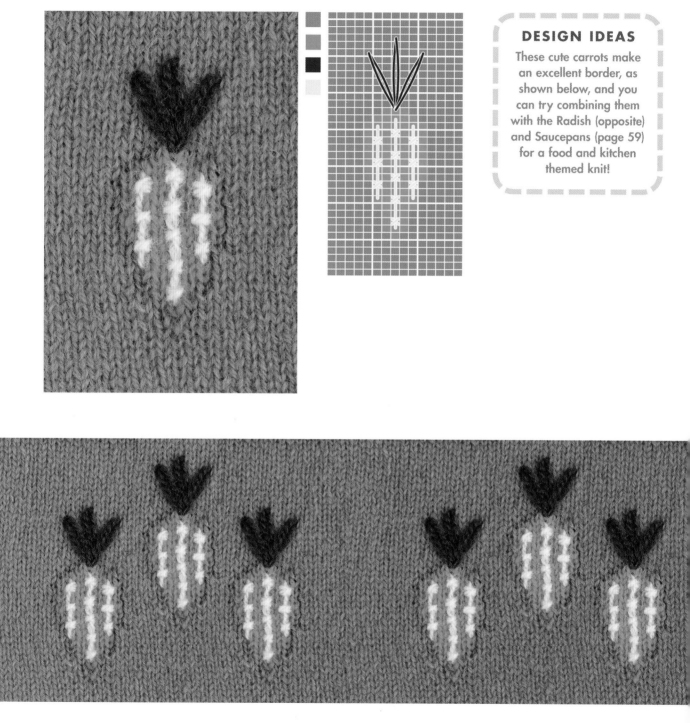

DESIGN IDEAS

These cute carrots make an excellent border, as shown below, and you can try combining them with the Radish (opposite) and Saucepans (page 59) for a food and kitchen themed knit!

Radish

This two-tone Radish with its simple embroidery makes a very versatile motif. Long straight stitches make the Radish tops and a few simple cross stitches decorate the radish itself. Use the Radish as a single sweet motif for a baby's bib, hat, and jacket or a prettily placed pocket on a little dress.

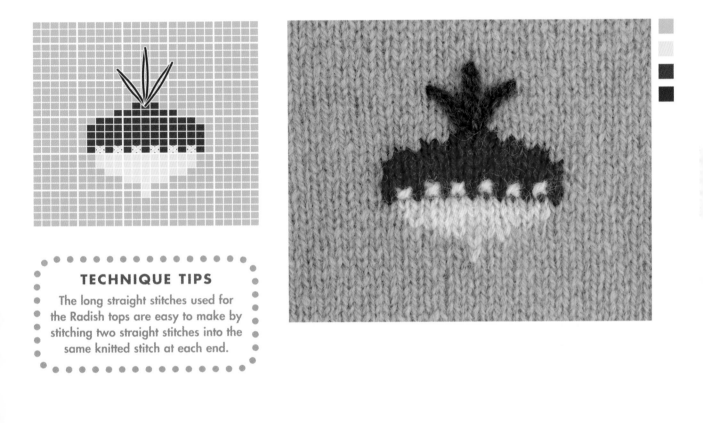

TECHNIQUE TIPS

The long straight stitches used for the Radish tops are easy to make by stitching two straight stitches into the same knitted stitch at each end.

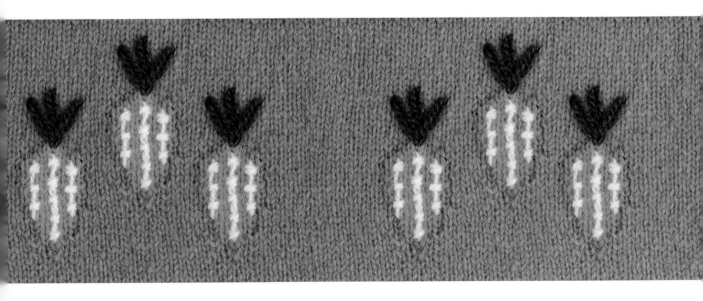

Wild Flower

Big, wild, and fabulous, this stylized and eye-catching flower would make a stunning addition to a little girl's dress or top. Repeated in rows the Wild Flower makes a wonderfully exuberant border. You could try reversing the colors, with a light ground and darker flower for variation.

Garden Flowers

These pretty Garden Flowers with their colorful cross stitches and French knots will make lovely designs for a little girl's jacket or bag. They would also look very sweet decorating a pair of socks—remember to flip the chart for the second sock so that the motifs look balanced.

Round Flower

The Round Flower was inspired by a richly embroidered band of flowers found on a Polish peasant skirt. With the bright, textured French knots emphasizing its roundness, this jolly design would look great on little skirts, belts, hats, and socks. The birds look very happy in their flowery socks!

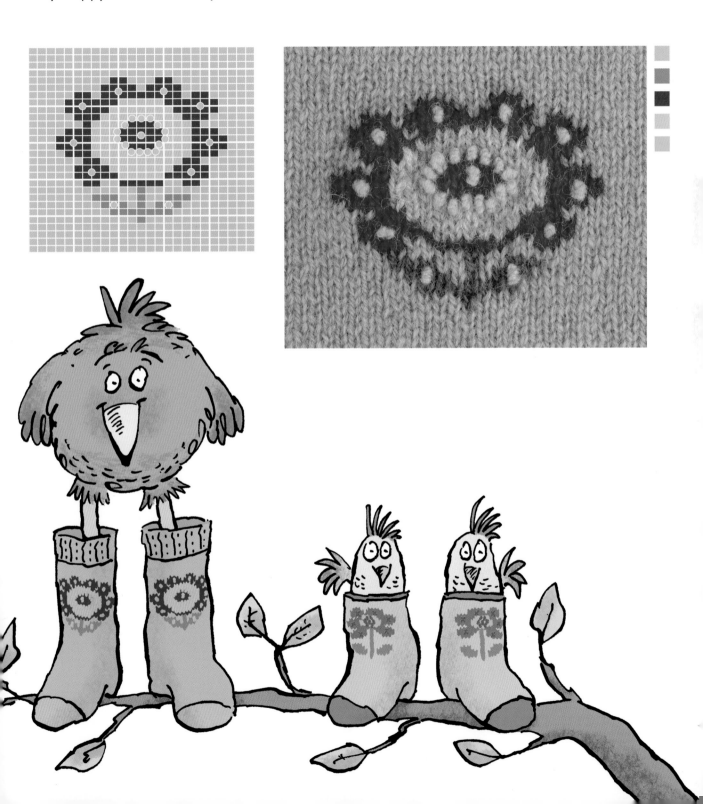

Harebell

Delicate and charmingly old fashioned, these pretty Harebells look lovely on any baby knits or girls' dresses. They make a great border or could be worked as shown here—vertically—on a pair of socks or bag. Flip the chart to alter the direction of the Harebell.

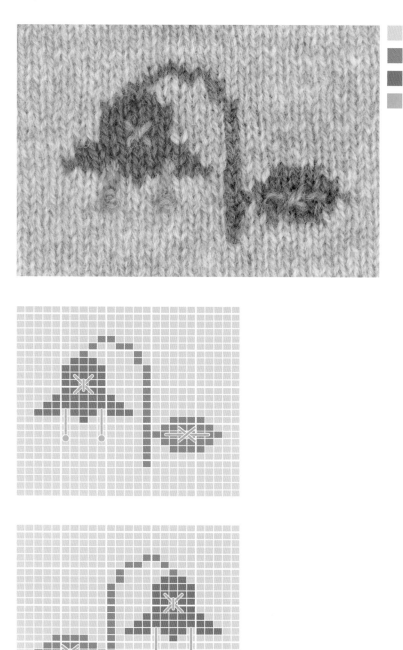

Little Garden Flowers

These Little Garden Flowers are really very useful and versatile motifs as they are bold enough to use on their own, small enough to repeat as sweet and dainty borders, and simple enough to combine well with other motifs. They would look gorgeous combined with the simple geometrics (page 104), the Little Birds (page 46), and Toadstool (page 41).

simple geometrics (page 104), the Little Birds (page 46), and Toadstool (page 41).

DESIGN IDEAS

As shown on the sweater below, lovely all-over patterns and borders can be created by combining these two Little Garden Flower motifs together.

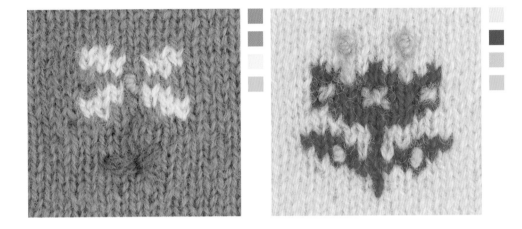

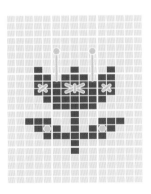

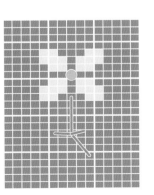

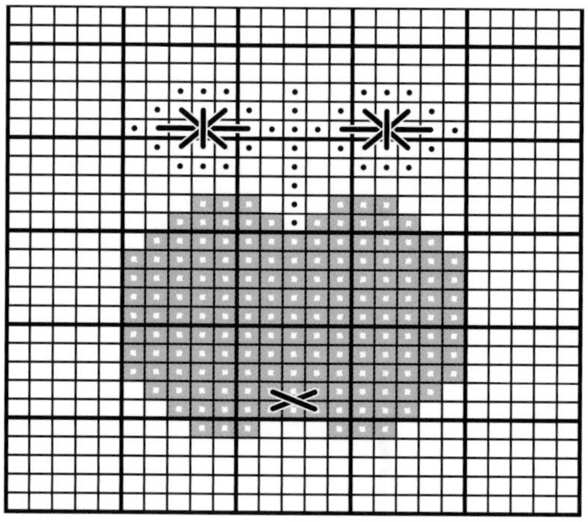

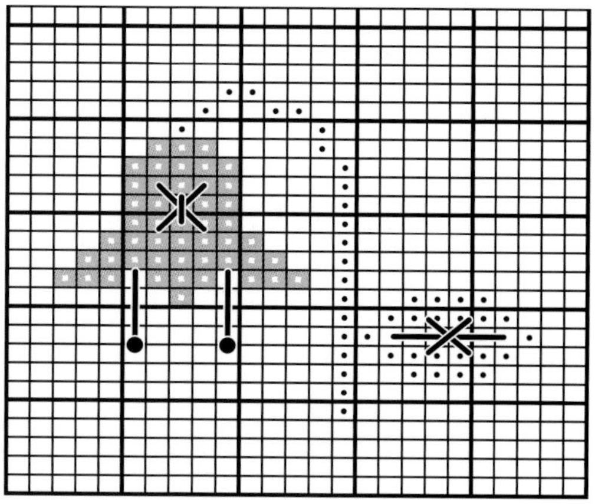

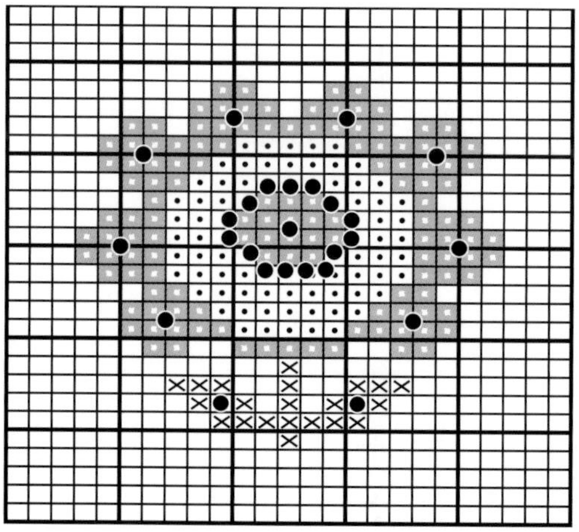

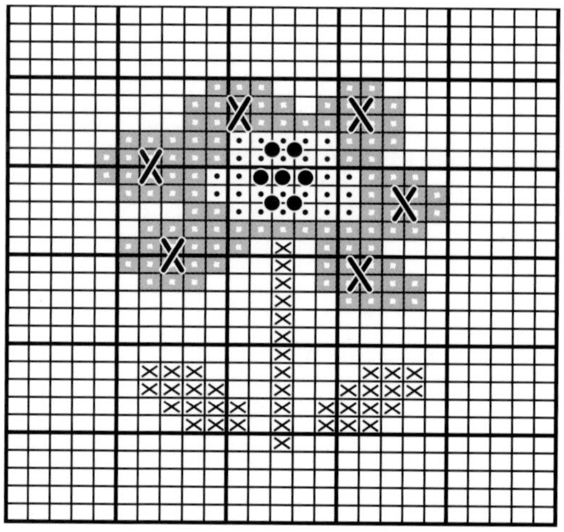

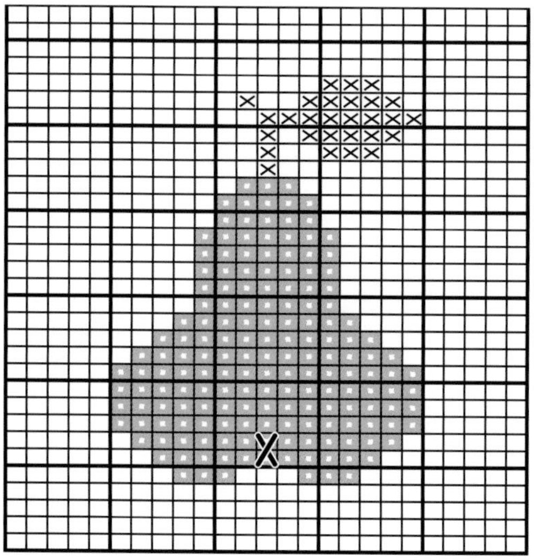

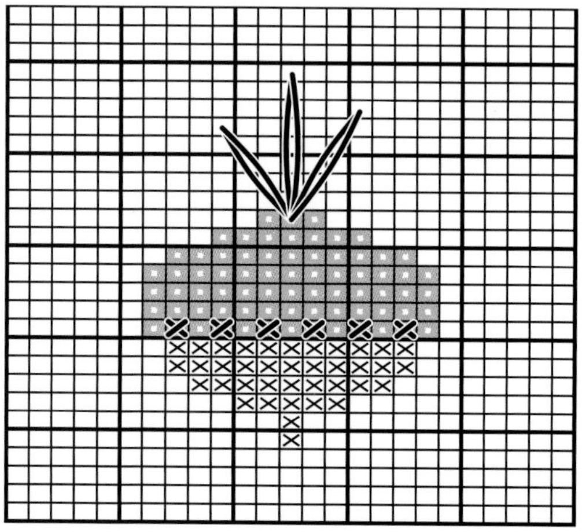

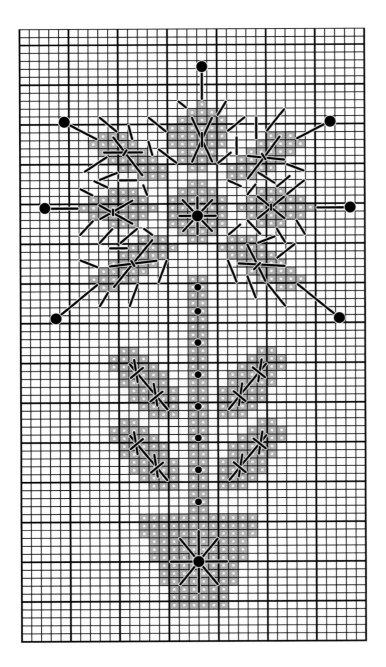

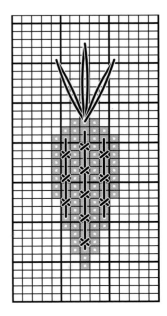

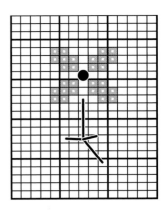

Transport and Toys

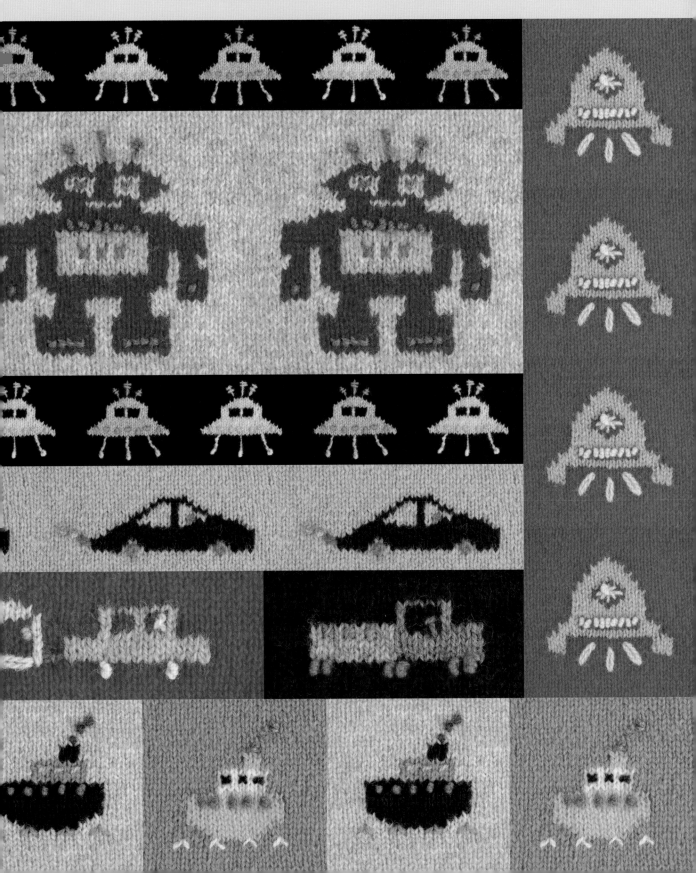

Boats

These jolly little Boats will add a nautical and seaside feel to knits for both girls and boys. Plenty of bright embroidery stitches, such as French knots, straight stitches, and cross stitches, all add texture, color, and detail. Repeat them in rows on a beach bag or position one on the bib of a sunsuit just like the little girl is wearing (right).

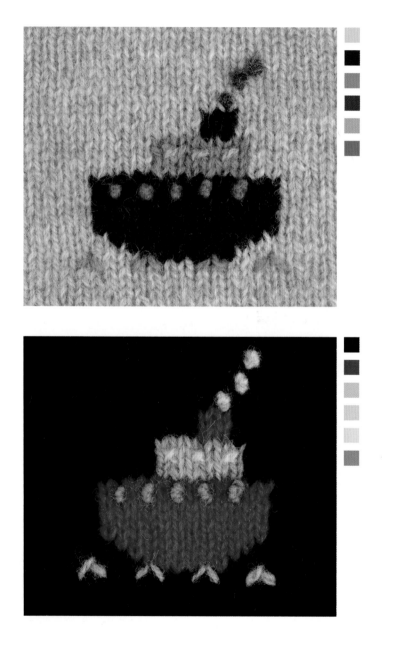

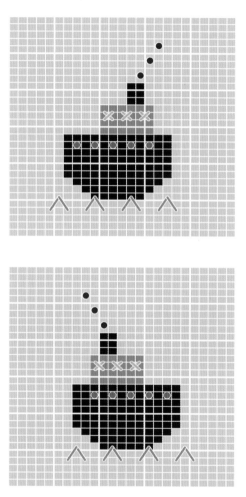

DESIGN IDEAS

Why not knit this motif up in a thicker wool yarn and use it for patchwork squares in alternating colors for a beach rug? Or try a cotton yarn for summer tops, beach bags, or sun hats.

Big Digger

Little boys will love to wear a sweater with a Big Digger on it. The Big Digger combines well with other motifs such as the Big Cars (opposite), Cars and Caravans (page 84), and Trucks (page 85) so why not try making a bright colorful blanket, tank tops, or sweater using all these motifs together.

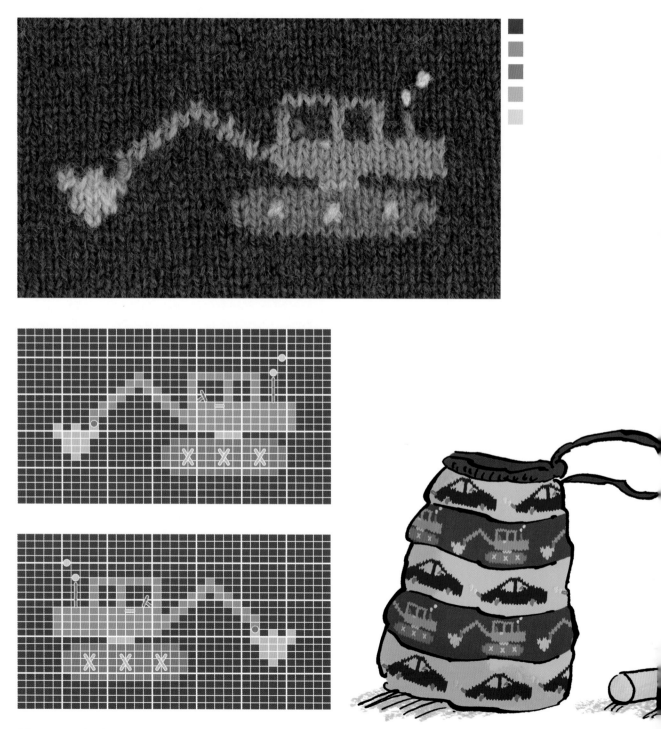

Big Cars

Simple and stylish, the Big Cars motif is a classic nursery design which is easily knitted in one color with an embroidered steering wheel, exhaust pipe, and fumes, and big bullion knots as wheels. It will combine brilliantly with other motifs, especially the Big Digger (opposite), so why not get organized and knit a useful toy bag like the one below?

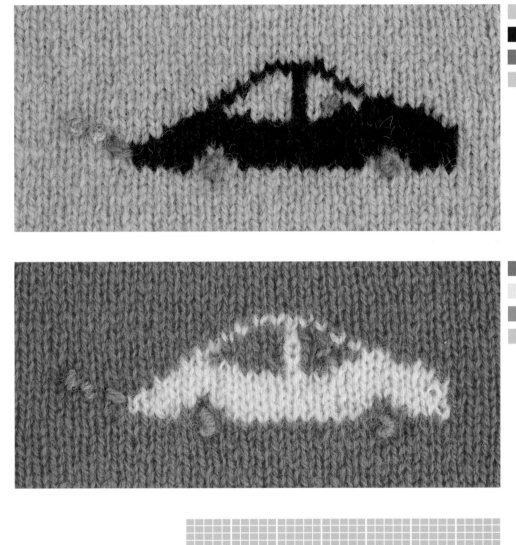

Cars and Caravans

Vintage wooden children's puzzles were the inspiration for these quaint, quirky, and slightly old-fashioned looking Cars and Caravans. They make delightful decorations for nursery knits and you can use the motif as a border or in bands of pattern, flipping the chart to change the direction they are traveling in. Happy vacation!

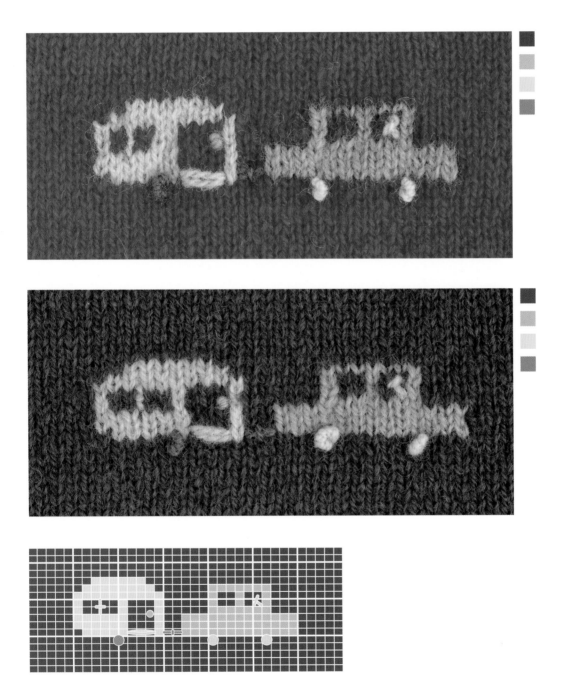

Trucks

Combine this cute little Truck motif with one of the colorful geometric borders (page 104) and you will have a superb design for a baby's outfit, cap, or crib blanket. Small and simple, the Trucks are quick to knit and with just a few embroidery stitches they are soon finished and ready to go!

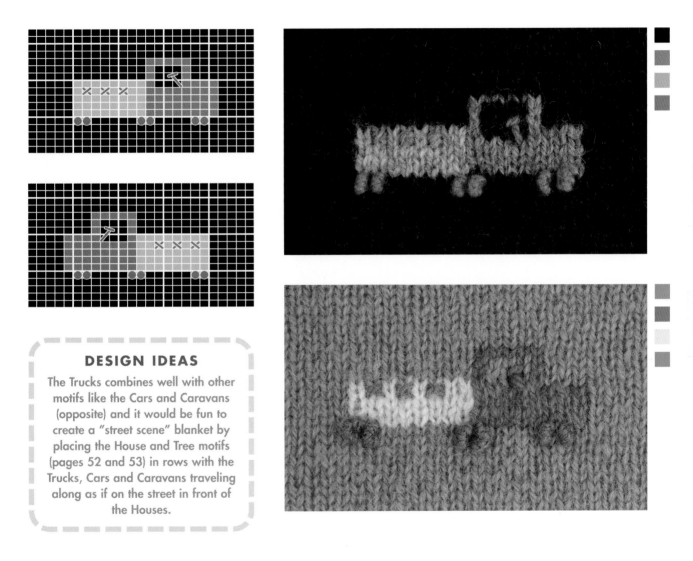

DESIGN IDEAS

The Trucks combines well with other motifs like the Cars and Caravans (opposite) and it would be fun to create a "street scene" blanket by placing the House and Tree motifs (pages 52 and 53) in rows with the Trucks, Cars and Caravans traveling along as if on the street in front of the Houses.

Robots

Robot motifs are a firm favorite with all children and these not-so-very-scary looking Robots with their embroidered feet, hands, eyes, dials, and antennae would look great striding across blankets, dresses, hats, or sweaters.

DESIGN IDEAS

Use different colored Robots on the same colored backgrounds or just repeat the Robots as shown here to make a fantastic blanket.

Spaceships

Science story books from the 1950s inspired these retro-style looking Spaceships, which make great single motifs for boys' bags or pencil cases. Combined with the Rockets (opposite) and other motifs like the Robots (pages 86 and 87) and the Man in the Moon (page 55), these Spaceships make an exciting outer space theme for any knits.

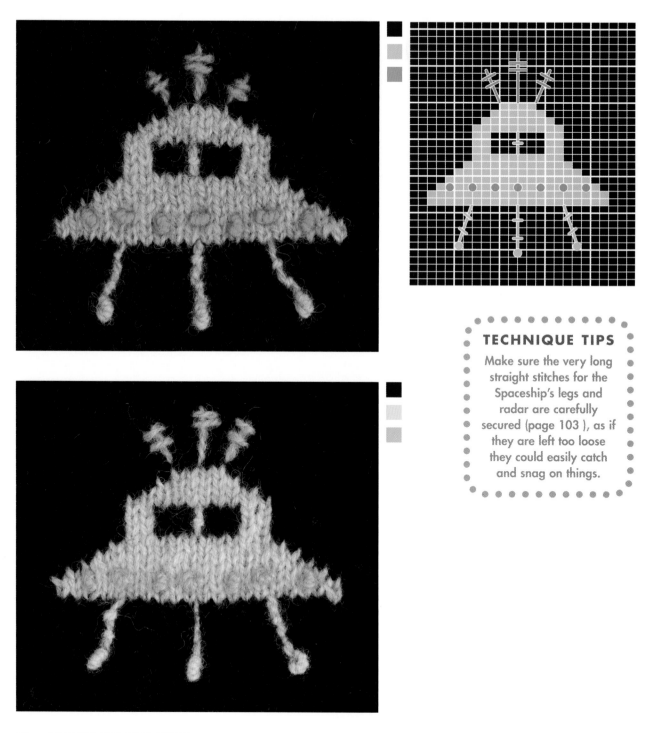

TECHNIQUE TIPS
Make sure the very long straight stitches for the Spaceship's legs and radar are carefully secured (page 103), as if they are left too loose they could easily catch and snag on things.

Rockets

Most kids love playing with toy rockets and now they can have their very own rocket knitted onto pockets, bags, blankets, hats, and just about anything! The Rockets are easily knitted in two colors with French knots, long straight stitches and a big, bright star stitch as decoration.

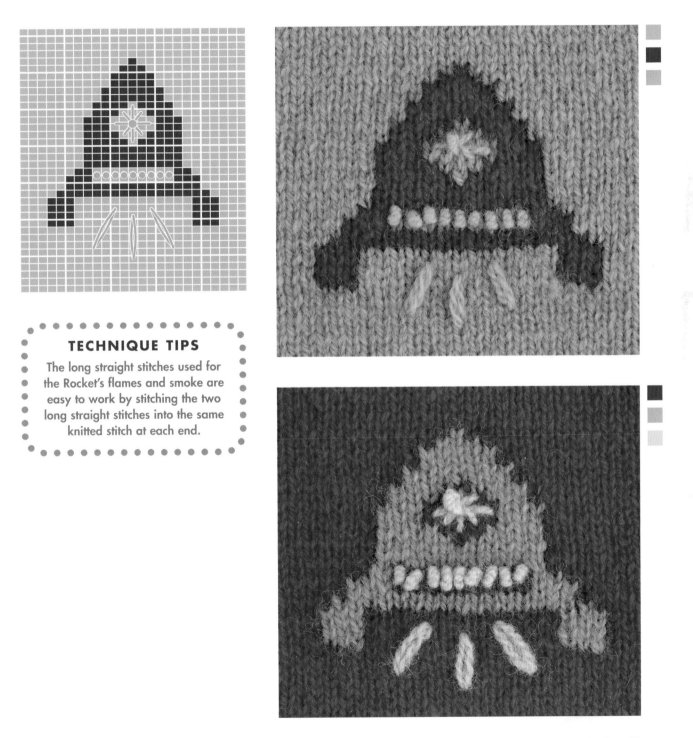

TECHNIQUE TIPS

The long straight stitches used for the Rocket's flames and smoke are easy to work by stitching the two long straight stitches into the same knitted stitch at each end.

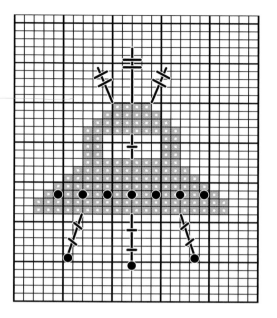

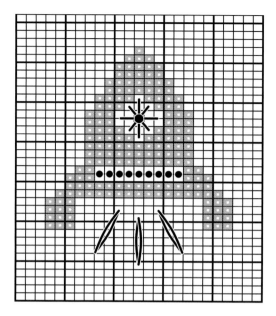

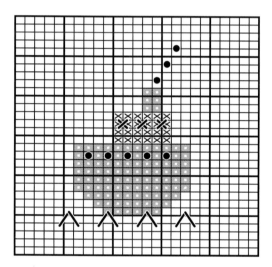

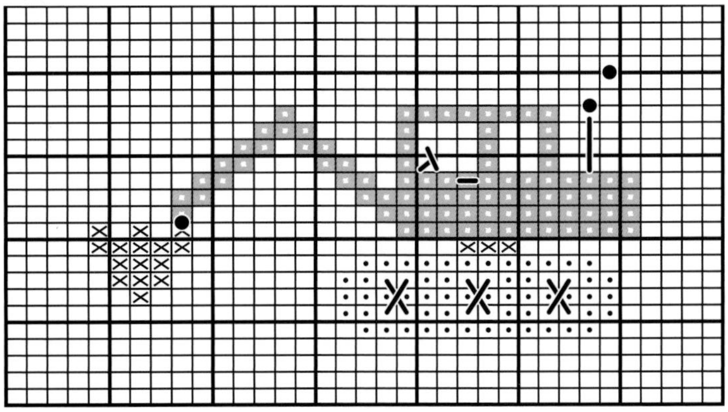

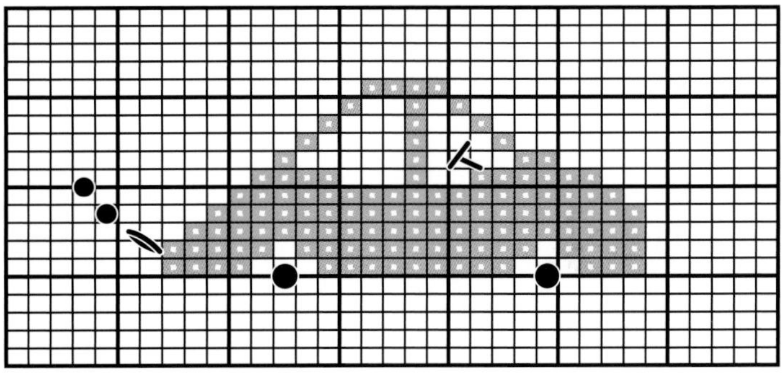

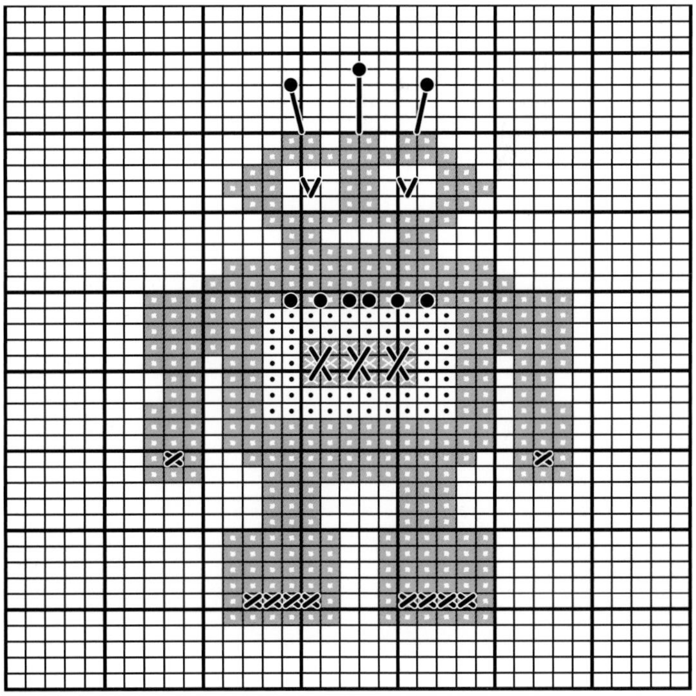

Knitting with Intarsia

Intarsia is a technique used when knitting single motifs or single areas of color and pattern. No fancy stitch work is involved—if you can knit and purl, you can do Intarsia.

Importantly, the different colored yarns needed for the motif are not carried across the back of the work and woven in as you would for continuous patterned knitting such as Fair Isle, but are used individually as required instead.

These new yarns can be wound into small individual balls or bobbins for each color in each motif (page 96). When you join a new yarn you "twist" it around the previous yarn worked to ensure a seamless, even join (page 94). These yarn lengths are always held at the back of the knitting and once the motif is finished they are cut and then darned

carefully into the back of the work. The largest amount of yarn is usually the one used for the background of the knitting and you may find you need to join in a new length of this same color. If you do, try to start a new length of the main color yarn at the beginning of a row rather than where it joins the motif, as this will minimize the extra ends and the resulting bulk around the motif.

The number of yarn ends that can accumulate around even a small motif can look alarming but do not be daunted! If you work slowly and patiently with your knitting and secure each new yarn length carefully as you go, you will certainly succeed.

The Intarsia technique prevents distortion or puckering around the motif, resulting in beautiful single-weight knitting.

Before You Begin

1. Make sure that the yarns you want to use are the same weight (pages 14–15).

2. Make sure that the colors of your choice will work together and are sufficiently contrasting (pages 10–11).

3. Study the chart of the motif that you want to use and make sure you have the correct number of colors that you will need.

4. Estimate how much of each color you will use and cut the lengths accordingly. Are you going to use more than one length of any yarn color?

5. Be generous with your yarn lengths as you will need sufficient to join them in plus sew them in securely on completion (page 100–101).

6. Wind the yarn lengths into small balls or into bobbins (page 96).

7. Have at hand a good pair of scissors and a pencil, and an eraser to use with the chart (pages 106–107).

8. Remember that small, tricky areas of color can be duplicate stitched afterward (pages 98–99).

9. Check each completed row against the chart (pages 106–107).

10. Think ahead to the next row—anticipate and calculate!

The Intarsia Technique

1 Calculate exactly where you want the motif to be placed on your knitting and mark the first and last stitch accordingly. (These step by step photos illustrate starting the motif on the right side of the knitting, on a knit row.)

2 With the right side facing you, knit to the first motif marker. Using the new motif yarn, knit the first stitch of the motif. Insert the needle in the second stitch and cross the main yarn *OVER* the new motif yarn to secure it. Continue to knit the second stitch.

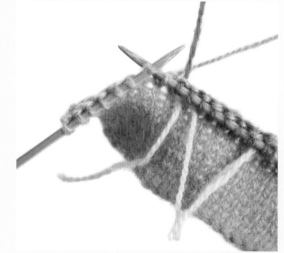

3 The two yarns are now twisted together and the main yarn is secured. Continue to knit to the end of the motif.

4 At the end of the motif, join in a new length of the main yarn and knit one stitch. Before you knit the second stitch, cross the motif yarn *OVER* the main yarn to secure it.

5 Before you start your second row (a purl row), take a look at the back of the knitting. You will see that where the yarns have been crossed over each other at the beginning and end of the motif there is a smooth, seamless join without gaps or holes.

6 Purl to the beginning of the motif and as you purl the first stitch of the motif cross the motif yarn *OVER* the main yarn to secure it.

7 When you have finished the motif, purl the first stitch with the main yarn and cross the main yarn *OVER* the motif yarn to secure it.

8 Continue to knit and purl each row in this way, always crossing the yarns one over the other at the beginning and end of the motif. The photo shows that when you cross the yarns they become twisted together at each edge of the orange square, creating a seamless join.

Making a Bobbin

Using bobbins will make Intarsia knitting much easier as they are a clever and efficient way of keeping all your yarns tidy and organized.

1 Wrap the yarn around your thumb and little finger in a figure eight movement.

2 Cut the yarn leaving a short tail and wrap this several times, fairly tightly, around the middle of the bobbin.

3 Thread the tail of yarn onto a wool needle and secure it under the wrapped yarn.

4 Carefully remove the bobbin from your hand. Pull the unwrapped end of yarn to release the working yarn.

Fair Isle Knitting

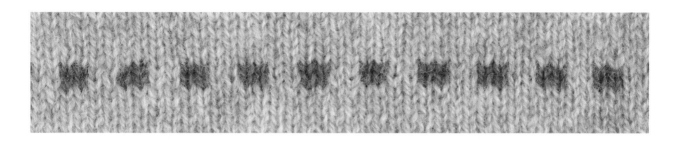

Fair Isle, or Stranded Knitting, is a technique usually used for seamless in the round (circular) knitting with colored continuous patterning. Two colors are used in most rounds and the strand not in use is carried across the wrong side of the knitting and woven in as required by the pattern, creating a double thick fabric. Traditionally the number of stitches between the different colors is quite small, usually not more than 5.

You can use the Fair Isle technique when knitting motifs, but it is only ever used over very small areas where only two colors are being used. Occasionally it can be combined with the Intarsia method when small, two-colored areas appear. For example, I would recommend that the Little Bird (page 46) is knitted using the Fair Isle technique as it is knitted in two colors and is only 7 stitches wide and 6 rows deep. Similarly the central patterned

area of the Hearts (page 43) and Star (page 44) can be knitted with the Fair Isle technique whilst the Intarsia technique is used for the main motif outline. It is best to restrict the use of the Fair Isle technique, however, as the resulting woven-in areas of knitting may look lumpy and bulky compared with the smoother, flatter areas of Intarsia knitting.

Before using the Fair Isle technique for a motif you need to consider carefully if the method is compatible with the color combinations that you are using, as dark colors carried behind very light colors may show through and spoil the motif. Also, if the motif requires more than two colors to be used in one row, the carrying and weaving in of the yarns may become quite complicated. Always try to maintain an even gauge (tension) and make sure that the areas knitted using the Fair Isle technique do not look pinched or too tight.

Duplicate Stitch

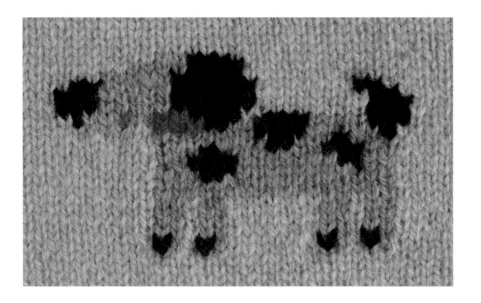

Duplicate stitch (also known as Swiss darning) is the perfect embroidery technique to use for small or single stitch areas of color on motifs. This technique is used specifically with knitting and as the name suggests the embroidery "duplicates" the knitted stitch. It is usually worked using the same weight yarn as the knitting as it is important to maintain an even and consistent gauge (tension).

One single duplicate stitch is ideal for an animal's eye such as Anil the Elephant (page 23) or Monette Mouse (page 30). It works well combined with other embroidery stitches, creating variety and definition such as on the Robots (page 86) and the Saucepans (page 59).

As the duplicate stitch doubles the thickness of the knitting where it is applied it can be used effectively to create subtle changes of texture and to highlight and define small areas of pattern. I would

recommend using duplicate stitch for Boris the Dog's eye, collar, and paws (page 25), as it not only helps to simplify the Intarsia but adds a slightly more realistic, two-dimensional effect.

Single Intarsia motifs are usually only used on flat knitting that is knitted in rows on two needles as, unless you use special techniques, you cannot knit single Intarsia motifs when creating seamless garments in the round. But if you want a single motif for a garment knitted in the round you could replicate the motif with duplicate stitch.

Duplicate stitch is also the perfect technique to use to cover up and correct mistakes on your motifs. If you make a mistake, do not start all over again; instead, consider using a few duplicate stitches in the appropriate colored yarn to disguise the error. It may help save a lot of hard work.

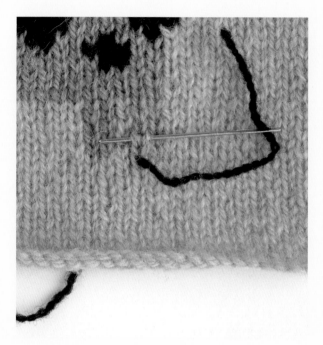

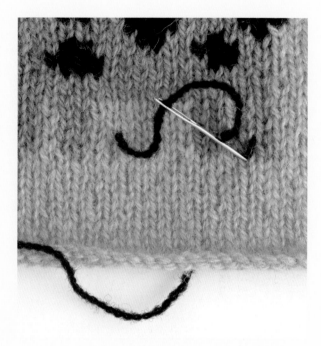

1 Thread a wool needle with yarn of the chosen color and correct weight, and take it from the back of the knitting through to the front at the base of the stitch that you want to duplicate. Pass the needle *behind* the stitch above.

2 Pull the needle through and following the "V" shape of the knitted stitch, pass the needle back through the base of the same stitch.

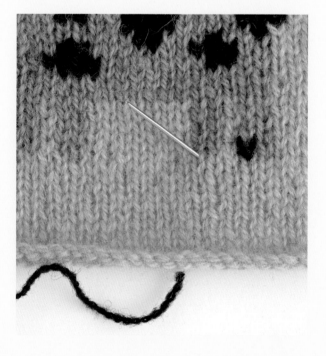

3 The Duplicate stitch is complete. Maintain an even and consistent gauge (tension) by slightly stretching the knitted fabric after each duplicate stitch is made.

Finishing

1 When you have finished the motif you will need to untangle the yarns or bobbins and cut each of them to 4in (10cm). Do not cut the yarn too short as you will need to sew in each one to the stitches on the back of the motif to secure it, making sure that the darned-in yarns do not show through onto the right side of the knitting.

2 Thread the yarn end onto a wool needle and pass the needle under and over several of the nearest stitches around the outside of the motif. Take the yarn back through a few of the same stitches of the motif to make sure it is secure and will not come undone. It is important to do this as neatly and carefully as possible so as to minimize any bulky areas that may make the motif appear uneven and also to make sure that there is no "show through" of colors from the front of the knitting.

3 Cut the yarn ends leaving a tiny tail of about $3/4$–1in (2–3cm). This will allow for ease when washing the knitted piece. Any unsightly ends can then be snipped off once the knitting has dried.

Washing and Pressing

Whatever yarns you use, all knitted motifs will benefit greatly from being lightly pressed on the back of the knitting with a warm iron over a damp cloth. The motif should look as flat and seamless as possible. If you are using wool to knit with, I recommend hand-washing the knitted piece in warm, soapy water, rinsing it well to remove all traces of soap, and then rolling it in a towel to squeeze out the excess moisture before laying it flat to dry.

Embroidery Stitches

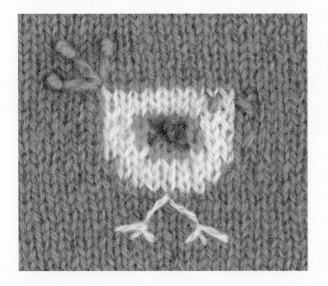

Simple embroidery stitches will enhance any motif and are an ideal way of combining extra color, texture, and detail. All the stitches I have used are easily made and the knitting provides a perfect even grid to work onto. Often only very small amounts of colored yarn are required to work a few simple embroidery stitches so never throw away ends of left-over yarn as you could start to accumulate different colors and weights to use for embroidery.

No matter how hard you try to replicate the embroidery, each motif or character may end up looking slightly different—the position of the legs or beaks may never be exact and each will be unique. The charted embroidery is there as a guide!

Your embroidery may not be perfect, but the imperfections are all part of the charm, and your garment will have the unique, lovely qualities and characteristics of being made by hand.

Star Stitch

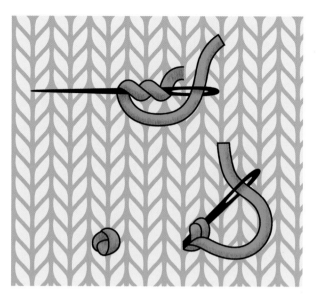

French Knot

Bullion Knot

Long Stitch (with Securing Stitch)

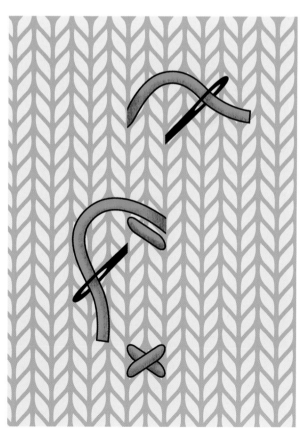

Cross Stitch

Geometric Motifs

Very simple, equally proportioned, and continuous patterns are perfect to use as borders to complement the motifs. You can use the colors in the motifs or complementary or contrasting colors for these borders, using the border either as a single row of highlight color or repeating it in a variety of patterns and colors.

Geometrics can help to balance the color and the patterns that you are using in your garment and can be used either to connect or separate the motifs. Small, continuous, two-colored patterns like these can be knitted using the Fair Isle technique (page 97).

You could experiment with your own simple geometric patterns, as there are endless variations—many more than I have shown here. A good source of ideas for designs can be found in traditional folk art and embroidery books.

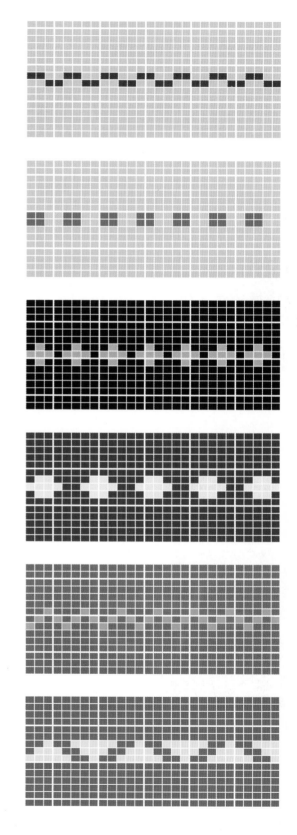

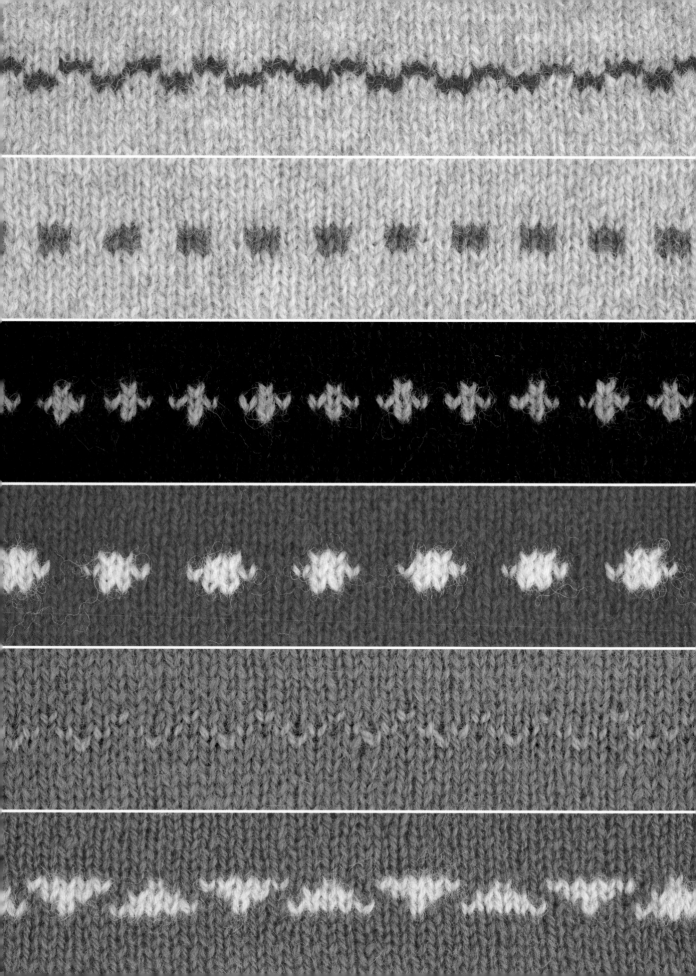

Reading Charts

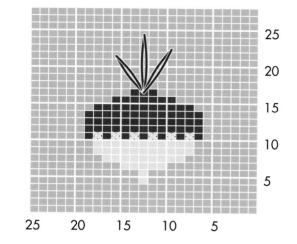

When knitting motifs on two needles you read the chart from right to left on the knit rows (the right side of the knitting) and from left to right on the purl rows (the wrong side of the knitting). If you are knitting a continuous pattern in the round on a circular needle using the Fair Isle technique you read the chart from right to left on every round.

Each square on the chart represents one stitch, and often one square contains both knitting and embroidery information for that stitch.

One row on the chart represents one row of knitting, and you may find it easier if you number the rows on your own chart.

The black and white charts at the end of each chapter are ideal for photocopying and using as a chart to work from or you could draw up your own chart using the custom-made grids (pages 108–109). This way you can separate the embroidery information from the knitted information. Either way, I would recommend that you keep track of your knitting by drawing a pencil line across each row as you finish it.

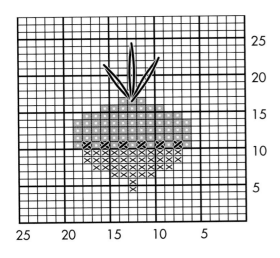

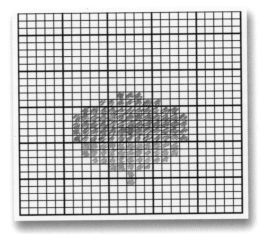

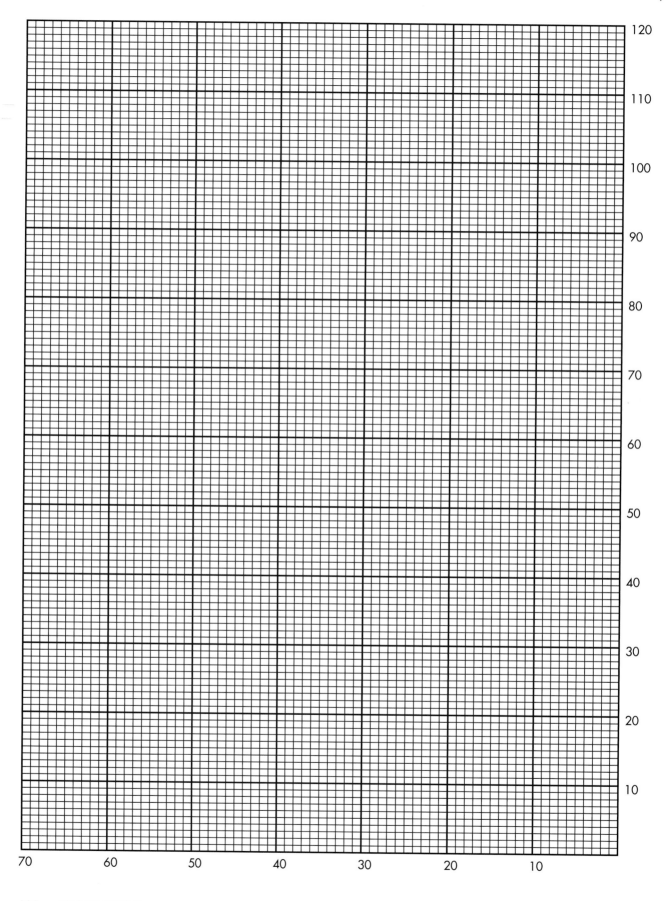

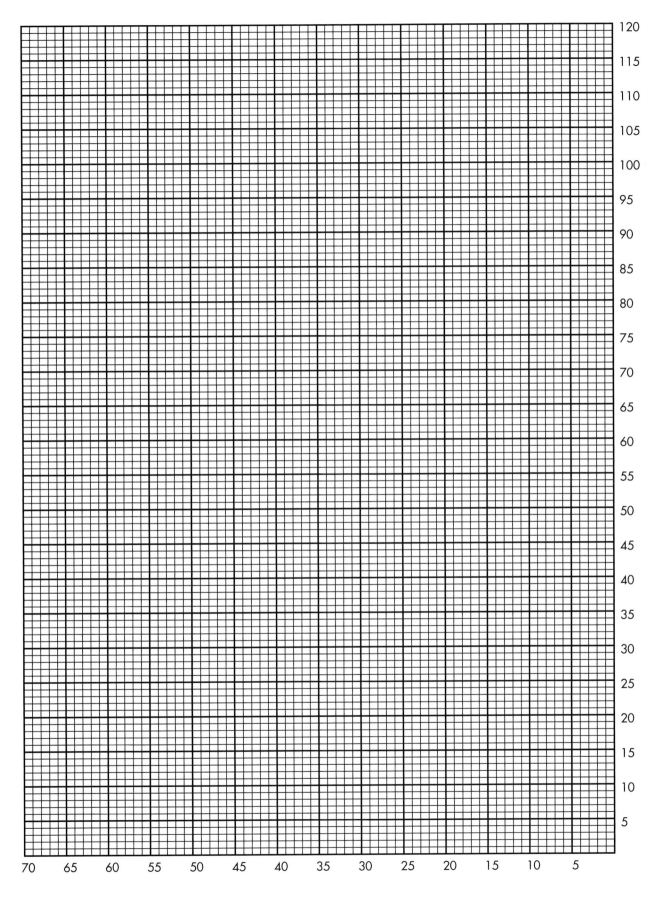

Yarns and Stockists

The yarns used to knit the motifs in this book are all by Jamieson & Smith.

Jamieson & Smith
90 North Road
Lerwick
ZE1 0PQ
Shetland Isles
www.shetlandwoolbrokers.co.uk

Dale of Norway
4750 Shelburne Road, Suite 2
Shelburne, VT 05482
USA
www.dale.no

Ístex
PO Box 140
270 Mosfellsbær
Iceland
www.istex.is

Schoolhouse Press
6899 Cary Bluff
Pittsville, WI 54466
USA
www.schoolhousepress.com

Westminister Fibers Inc.
165 Ledge Street
Nashua, NH 03060
USA
www.westministerfibers.com

Rowan Yarns
Green Lane Mill
Holmfirth
West Yorkshire
HD9 2DX
UK
www.knitrowan.com

Index of Motifs

Acknowledgments

Many thanks to Jamieson & Smith for their beautiful yarn, everyone at Trafalgar Square Books and Search Press, and to all involved in the making of this book—it couldn't have happened without you!